Praise for *The Kindness Games*

"We all need a little dose of [ ] The Kindness Games delivers just stories, readers dive deep into the motivations behind acts of kindness, often discovering that the journey of gratitude can be more transformative than the act itself. *The Kindness Games* beautifully underscores that kindness is a choice, leaving a lasting impact on the reader. Powerful, personal, and practical — highly recommended!"

— Shamane Tan, Chief Growth Officer, Sekuro, Founder, Cyber Risk Meetup, Author of *Cyber Mayday and the Day After*

"If you're awaiting your big moment to make a difference, you're missing out on how meaningful progress gets done through habitual and strategic kindness — in your sphere of influence. *The Kindness Games* is a quick, easily digestible how-to compilation containing relatable stories and handy chapter summary reminder boxes that will catalyze your kindness routine. Why? Because it matters. It's how you make a difference."

— S. Lucia Kanter St. Amour, VP of UN Women, San Francisco, Law Professor, Author of *For the Forces of Good: The Superpower of Everyday Negotiation*

"Dive into a heartwarming journey of self-discovery and human connection in *The Kindness Games*. Explore the captivating world where kindness isn't just an act, but a choice we make. Join the protagonist as they embrace the contagious ripple effect of kindness, realizing that it takes courage to be kind in a world that sometimes feels harsh. Through challenges and triumphs, learn how being kind isn't just about others, but a powerful tool to shape your mindset and transform your life. *The Kindness Games* is a touching reminder of our shared responsibility to uplift one another."

— Dr. Dean McKay, Founding Partner and Chief Value Creator, Transformex

"Tim and Lee created a movement with The Kindness Games on LinkedIn — right smack in the middle of when the world stopped moving. As Kindness Games Alumnus #41, I instinctively ask curiosity questions (see Chapter 5!) to approach with kindness first. This movement fueled me to be intentional with kindness. One person at a time, we can fight for a kinder world. I highly recommend you pick up *The Kindness Games*, which teaches us through the stories and authenticity of people, and join the life-changing crusade."

— Jennifer Stanford, CEO, Trust Coach, and Servant Leader of Emergent Performance Solutions, a Change Management Consulting Firm

"Expressing kindness is an incredibly powerful behavior. After all, we live in a world where acts of kindness are too few and far between. Yet, when reading *The Kindness Games*, I was deeply touched by the transformation that took place within TKG participants. Their journeys motivated them to show up authentically — their stories will inspire you to do the same."

— Dean Hallett; President, Hallett Leadership; Author, *The Missing Piece: How Successful Companies Develop High-Performance Cultures*

"*The Kindness Games* is more than a book and more than a game. TKG is a call to action, a demand for healing, and a demonstration of the power of being kind. While *The Kindness Games* contains a wonderful collection of stories testifying to the process' impact on those who completed it, it is much more. *The Kindness Games* is a guidebook and reference for introspection and personal enlightenment. On the other side of this decade of change is a new world that requires new leaders who are compassionate, vulnerable, and comfortable with being uncomfortable."

— Scot Walker, Investigations Leader, Protection Futurist

THE
Kindness Games

How a Single Post Changed Our Mindset About Community

by Lee Oughton and Tim Wenzel

Published by How2Conquer
Atlanta, Georgia
www.how2conquer.com

How2Conquer is an imprint of White Deer Publishing, LLC
www.whitedeerpublications.com

First edition, October 2023
Ebook edition created 2023

Illustrations and cover design by Telia Garner
Edited by Emily M. Owens, Lauren Kelliher

Library of Congress Control Number: 2023945510

Print ISBN 978-1-945783-21-0
Ebook ISBN 978-1-945783-29-6

I aspire to have a clear conscience when I tell them that I Lead with Kindness. I aspire to heal my community and change the world by intentionally spreading kindness each day with each interaction.

Because it is right.

Contents

A Tribute to a Kindness Warrior

We take this opportunity to celebrate the life of a wonderful man, loving husband, servant leader, veteran of foreign wars, and one of the kindest humans to have roamed this planet. Steve Donofrio was never an average man. He graced everyone he met with an abundance of passion, drive, and determination.

Donofrio, Steve, Stevey D blessed us all with his advice and attention to detail. He was a man who never left you alone, who never allowed you to suffer in silence, who always put others before himself — who would put it all on the line, just to see another smile. We wish we could have more time.

Steve, our friend, everyone's friend, you will be sorely missed. We will forever cherish the wonderful memories of the times we spent together. You had a heart of gold, where everything and everyone you were able to touch with your warmth and generosity always prospered and glowed so brightly. This glow was seen like a ray of light during your times in Japan and India, where you put the spotlight on beautiful people by showing the world their capabilities through encouraging future leaders and fostering their talents.

You truly were a saint. Now it's your time to rest and basque in the glory up above. May you feast like a King, drink like a Viking warrior, and soar like an eagle gliding through the skies above.

Your Kindness remains with us.

All our love,
Your Fellow Kindness Crusaders

Foreword

What would change if kindness were our default over anxiety, fear, resentment, and even entitlement? What would change if we understood our impact on others, if we understood the power of our presence among everyone in our sphere of influence? And what would change if we discovered that we have far more that unites us than that which divides us? In a world where darkness and dread are often the defaults, imagine being brought into a light that exposes us in all the best ways. The Kindness Games is a call to something more real, more courageous, more human, and more whole. It's much more than a bunch of people who choose to express gratitude to others at an intentional cadence. It's so much more than oversimplified vulnerability. It's an invitation to see our world differently than the cultural narrative that has plagued us for so long.

This is the story of unlikely friendships and unlikely players in a movement of kindness. This is the story of a summons to join community. The Kindness Games encourages us to recapture the original intent of our lives, to experience purpose more deeply, to support others on the same mission, and to reach for humanity again. It's not a story of people with their heads in idealized clouds made of ponies and fairy tales, but one of real and courageous people showing gratitude amid our setbacks and disappointments. While movements, brands, and logos will come and go, The Kindness Games will continue beyond its name. It started as a simple challenge to express gratitude on video to people who made an impact. It has since become something that called us home.

Many of these contributors have become my dear friends. It has been my great pleasure to be in their corner as they go on their journeys. These are strong and humble humans who authored the pages you are about to read. They are benevolent lions in a world that sorely needs them.

Leading with kindness takes courage that starts with an invitation. In a world where there is so much blame, resentment, and finger pointing, The Kindness Games community invites us each to see it differently and to begin with grace, gratitude, and appreciation. This community isn't offering you a formula for success, but a bid to become whole again. The leaders of this movement asked us, "Will you lead the healing of your community?" To my friends who have so courageously and authentically told their stories here I say, "Yes." I see you, I am with you, and I am profoundly grateful for the prompt to join you.

Dr. Rob McKenna
Founder & CEO, WiLD Leaders

Inspired by Kindness

Dear Reader,

We invite you to go back in time with us to the tumultuous period that was the beginning of the COVID-19 quarantine. Now that we've made it a few years past what seemed like an alternate reality, it can be difficult to reckon with what we've lived through. Remember the isolation? Fear? Heightened anxiety on a global scale? That's when The Kindness Games was born.

September 2, 2020 — it was almost six full months after the world shut down in mid-March 2020.

I inserted my single-use key card into the reader and dragged my baggage into my hotel room. The door closed behind me with a hollow thud. I dropped my bags, took a shower to freshen up after the 15-hour travel day, then wandered to the chair and sat down. It was so dark outside, which ironically was how I was beginning to feel as the weight of a second two-week COVID-19 quarantine began to settle upon me. I turned on the TV. What I saw caused the heaviness to grow. As I switched channels, I had a thought on loop in my head, one that was foreign to me: "I don't know how well I'll survive this."

I remembered my wife's worry when I left for the airport and the preparations we made together to prepare for the possibility of violence in our neighborhood while I was gone again. I couldn't keep busy enough to shut it out. I was going to be *alone* with my thoughts and the TV for two weeks. I was feeling depressed for the first time in my entire life. My life had been tumultuous, I've been surrounded by crisis and publicity and uncertainty, yet this hotel room was going to be my breaking point?

To be fair, it wasn't just the media and culture clashes that were weighing me down. COVID-19 had many unforeseen consequences. In fact, on this trip on a video conference with my team, I broke down as I told them some of the things I was facing. Quite out of character for *this* "man of action."

I turned off the TV, opened my computer and a food delivery order page. I flipped to LinkedIn and saw a post from my friend Lee Oughton. I smiled and laughed to myself. *This guy is crazy! What a goof!*

Lee's post was an exuberant breath of fresh air. I'd never seen such an enthusiastic professional encouragement post. And not only that — he also congratulated those professionals on their willingness to learn new things and get outside of their comfort zones. His post was caring. He cared about the people he worked with and was willing to share that with the world.

I left a comment:

> Hey Lee Oughton! What if we did this every day? What if we spread kindness by lifting someone up for all to see?

Lee Oughton:

> Let's start tomorrow!

I sat back and thought about who I would choose to type up a small thought of gratitude for. Who would qualify, why would they qualify, and what meaningful theme could this take on? I thought about how in the United States, groups of people were being pitted against one another, resulting in violence and fear. How could we counter what was going on in mainstream media and make it an ongoing game?

Before going to bed, I responded to Lee:

> What if we made encouragement a competition? What if we one-upped each other with competitive kindness? I'm throwing down. Who's picking this up?

When I woke up, Lee was already well into his day and had tagged me on a LinkedIn post. A video?

> Tim and I have decided to have a competition to one-up each other in spreading kindness. Challenge accepted. Tim and I will be recording a video shouting out someone who deserves recognition each day for 30 days. . .

Videos? I didn't want to do videos! What did I have to say? Video content had to be way better than typing a few sentences. I still didn't know who my first post would be about. I was more overwhelmed than I was the previous night.

The hammer was dropped, and the challenge accepted.

We rumbled into the game, back and forth we gamely went, with Lee upping the ante right from the beginning by going big or going home through kindness video posts. It was such a great way to kick off. We encouraged new participants to join us on the wellness journey through some friendly competition.

The Kindness Games is an outlet for our participants to escape the mundane, tumultuous, and chaotic aspects of their lives, by allowing them to focus on special memories from their past and relive experiences that gave them so much joy and happiness. We get our participants to shine a light back on what really matters by being kind, gracious, showing gratitude to others, and being thankful for all that we have created and been given in our lives. Reframing minds is a great way to look at what we're doing with all our contributors, encouraging them to start their days through positive messaging physically and emotionally.

We started a life journey together, which was even more powerful considering we had never met in person, yet we had formed this bromance and blossoming relationship virtually.

How to Play

To play The Kindness Games, you really just need to follow five steps:

1. Commit to the 30-day journey.
2. Think about who you'll thank.
3. Think about what you'll say.
4. Set yourself a start date.
5. Start!

Commit to the 30-Day Journey

Embrace, understand, and envisage the power of the journey. This is where we push boundaries and take leaps of faith by being courageous and putting ourselves out there to a global audience. Though you may start in a potentially dark place, how to play is the platform that takes you through. It gives us a way out. In essence, it's hope.

Think about Who You'll Thank

Plan out and think of who you'd like to give thanks to on each daily post. Write the names down on a list. Look at what you want to achieve on your individual journey. Know that as you progress each day in a positive state of mind, you're bringing in the people around you: family, friends, partners, and spouses. They are also hearing your journey.

Starting your day with positivity will lift you up. The sense of community makes it easy to share your most challenging and vulnerable thoughts on a daily basis. You share not because you wanted someone to give you advice, but because you needed to get that off your chest. The community is always looking to give back to those going through a tough time. The process and alumni help those who don't know where their next step will take them.

Think about What You'll Say

Once you've chosen your daily kindness shout-outs, think what you'd like to say or record on those posts. Apply the subject and content narrative for each recipient. This is where your storytelling will come into play.

Alternatively, you can also take it day by day, lean into how you feel that day and who you want to give thanks to in that specific moment. Be more relaxed and feel your way into your TKG journey.

Your posts can either be written or video recordings. We would encourage you to take the video route, as we believe and as results have shown us the wellness journey is more beneficial face-to-face. Just also remember the power in the written word.

Set Yourself a Start Date

Assign the date you want to start. When Lee got the call from Tim, he felt a duty to support him. Tim explained TKG and where they could take it. The next day, Lee found his inspiration on a run. He found a nice spot by a beautiful lake and recorded his very first post. Find your day one and commit to it straight away.

Start!

Post consecutively for 30 days. Create a daily routine of waking up and thinking of your post. Think of who has impacted you the most. Set yourself up to succeed with small, achievable tasks. From the moment you open your eyes, use that positive mindset as the building blocks to accomplish your goals.

Tim's Tips:

- **One take.**
  No matter what.
- **No editing.**
  I don't know how, didn't want to learn, and don't have time.
- **Batch your content.**
  If you know you have travel coming up or will be inundated with appointments, meetings, or any other kinds of disruption, go ahead and batch a few shout-outs at once. If I'm going to record one video, why not record three? It only takes 15 minutes if you're doing one take.
- **Make a list.**
  Whether you're batching or not, maximize your time by creating a list of people you'd like to recognize. Change it up, make edits, whatever, but writing it down clears your mind, so you have the space to focus.
- **Change your clothes . . .**
  If you're batching, record days three, five, and seven. Tomorrow record four, six, and eight. It makes you look like you've changed clothes. You're welcome.
- **No notice, no permission.**
  The maximum effect on the person you're recognizing is the shock and overwhelming feeling of love and humility from being seen and appreciated. Also, some people will discourage you from doing it out of their own insecurity, but that's a limiting behavior. Don't share personal thoughts or conversations. Always ambush with kindness.

Leading with Kindness

Leading with kindness means choosing to give everyone unwarranted favor, or a reasonable benefit of the doubt. We never have to wonder how to treat anyone based on their role or position in society. We treat the employee the same as the CEO. This diminishes our internal situational conflict, and it gives our leadership and social style a manner of elegance. This type of philosophy is secretly esteemed by everyone and attracts others to you. People will be drawn to you because of how well you treat everyone, and success will follow.

Sure, we must learn from our mistakes. Yes, we need to take strategic steps to ensure we aren't hurt, but we can also forgive, set boundaries, and allow a new beginning. The truth is, if you say you recognize the imperfections of our common humanity, yet you will not extend grace, we cannot accept each other.

Together, we've come up with 10 simple tenets that define our philosophy on leading with kindness. You'll find these themes throughout the book.

Our Common Humanity

When we realize that our common humanity binds us tighter together than the forces which would divide us, we are stronger because of our shortcomings. Our flaws and reliance upon one another for strength and support highlight the beauty within our brokenness.

Holistic Kindness

Living a life of holistic kindness is counterculture to our world. It draws jeers, and people question your motives. It draws jealousy, and you're asked, "Why are you so happy?"

It unseats the existing balance of communities based on one interest, view, or likeness. They may try to exert a zero-sum game mentality on those who don't share their opinions.

Engage in Meaningful Conversations

If we are to heal our communities, we must be willing to have meaningful conversations, especially when they're difficult. We need to be curious and open to engaging respectfully during meaningful conversations. It's paramount to understanding who someone is, what their experiences have been, and how these have shaped their perception and ideas about life.

Assume Best Intent

Assuming the best intent in others allows us to let our guard down. Instead of wondering if they have an ulterior motive, we'll ask what they meant. Those with ill intentions will become uncomfortable having to explain their rationale to an open-minded, rational person. They'll begin to leave you alone.

Curiosity

In a world that tells us it's all about me, my identity, my goals, and my happiness — curiosity helps us focus on others. It provides the opportunity to learn about others, empathize with their experiences and struggles, and to allow them to be heard and feel known. This curiosity ironically helps us learn about ourselves, our perspectives, our biases, and gives us the chance to evaluate and improve.

Self-Control

Curiosity helps us regain and maintain our self-control. Choose to ask questions. Garner more information to help you understand where this attack is coming from, and what it's really about. Listen and be considerate of another's point of view. It'll help you stay calm while you regain your logical thought paths, shake yourself out of fight or flight mode, and choose how to react in the moment.

Mindfulness, Purpose, Grace

Grace has many definitions: unwarranted favor, goodwill, honor, and elegance of manner. We all fall short of our aspirations sometimes. Offense will come to us no matter how much we aspire to heal the communities around us. We will falter and offend, no matter our best intentions. Since this is inevitable, what if we extended grace to others when they do the same?

Acceptance

To have great relationships, form healthy communities, and heal broken ones, we must accept one another. Accept the beauty of our brokenness. When we are wronged, we must see our reflection in another's actions. Then we can use this acceptance to temper our reactions and ensure that our responses are measured, reasonable, and empathetic. There's risk and fear involved in knowing one another and to become known ourselves. What happens when we let go of risk and fear? We make room for kindness and connection.

The Elephant in the Room: Vulnerability

Our perspective on the world strongly affects who we believe we are, what we believe we can or cannot do, and ultimately how we interact with those around us. If we want better relationships, we need to examine ourselves and how we tend to understand the world by asking: Is this helpful? Does this belief serve me well? Does this worldview serve me well? Who am I becoming? Is this how I want to be remembered?

Life is a series of ups and downs. Life is a struggle. When asked to define the human condition, I keep coming back to this. We are defined by our high aspirations and our inability to fulfill them. One thing we all have in common is the certainty that we are imperfect. In the face of this truth, we all share another thing — hope. We share the hope that we can do better, build better, and leave the world around us better than we found it.

Meditating on "who you will become" has always been a worthwhile endeavor. At 21 years old, I was asked to do one of the most impactful reflective exercises I've ever done. In January 2003, I was serving in the National Guard when we were put on orders to prepare for the invasion of Iraq. As my squad and I prepared for isolated training, we did a mobilization exercise, a term for getting our affairs in order. We were asked to plan our funerals. This was how: we wrote down some things that we wanted at our funeral, people we might want to speak, things we might want read, and communicated those wishes to our families.

> **Try this: Consider how you want to be remembered by all you know and write a draft of your obituary.**

The exercise was practical, but the reflection brought sobriety and humility. Achieving great things is vanity if we alienate, injure, or destroy those around us.

I've re-written my obituary each decade since. Each time, I reflect on my journey, my accomplishments, and my failures. I add aspirations for my next decade. It's so powerful to take an honest account of where you are — the good and the bad — and set that as a new foundation and launching pad. By being vulnerable, we can acknowledge, accept, and forgive our past mistakes, or seek forgiveness for them. When we arrive fully and honestly in the present, we can dream again, mentally take a leap, and aspire to reach our next north star from where we are.

I reached out to Lee to ask if we could walk this journey of kindness and vulnerability together, because I needed someone to help lift me from the darkness. Lee and I resolved to post a video a day for 30 days, uplifting someone who had been kind to us or otherwise contributed kindness in the world.

When you make your list of people who have had a positive impact on your life, and you think about the kindness people have shown you, and you begin to post every day, you start to see the world in a different light. You are choosing to look for the good in people. You soften as you become more vulnerable with yourself and with others. You get to choose to surround yourself with and consume the kindness of others.

But then, the person you posted about sees it, they respond to your post, maybe they send you a private message or perhaps, they call you — like so many of the people I shouted out did. When they call you, you're often shocked. You expect a friendly call. A friend or even an acquaintance who's excited that you saw them and shared them to the world. But sometimes, the person on the other side of the phone is broken, crying, and allowing an avalanche of emotion to rush over you. You're shocked, but you listen. You learn the struggle behind their kindness. The pain they've had the entire time you've known them, yet you were unaware. Then you hear words like: "This is the nicest thing anyone has ever done for me. This is the best thing that's happened this year. I didn't know anyone saw me, and I felt so alone. Thank you."

In This Section

As you read the following stories from Bill, Heidi, and Sarah-Marie, consider each of their unique struggles with vulnerability.

Bill reckoned with stigma within the security industry — which Lee and I can relate to. Heidi worked up the courage to deal with emotional exposure in a professional setting. Sarah-Marie tore down the walls she had previously built to protect herself due to her past experiences.

Chapter 1: Moving Past Initial Reluctance

by Bill Massey, Law Enforcement Executive

Bill Massey is a law enforcement executive in the San Francisco Bay Area with over 27 years of public safety experience. Bill is a husband and father of three children, including one who is now a college graduate. He considers himself a lifelong learner and has embraced roles not only in leadership but also in executive coaching and mentoring, building virtual and in-person relationships across the globe.

I had absolutely no idea what an impactful community I would be joining in October 2020. I had been in public safety for 25 years and an instructor for an intensive leadership course for 17 of those. One of our primary themes in that leadership course was how a significant emotional event can define your life course, and participating in The Kindness Games led to one of those events for me. But before I tell you about that, let me take you back to the beginning of this journey.

In 2019, I began to explore secondary career options as I grew closer to being able to retire from my government job. I attended a course about transitioning from law enforcement to corporate security, and I left with a renewed passion. I began joining international and local security associations and deliberately connected with people on LinkedIn who seemed to share my sense of purpose. I first met Tim Wenzel at a San Francisco Bay Area ASIS (American Society for Industrial Security) corporate security meeting that same year. Over the following year, Tim and I spoke on a couple of occasions and traded a few messages via LinkedIn. Tim was, after all, a person in a corporate security position that was highly desirable: working for a social media company that was at the tip of the spear. Even though Tim was sought after by many people at the meetings, he always seemed to have time for anyone who genuinely engaged with him, including me.

The "Oh Fudge" Moment

On the morning of October 24, 2020, it happened. Tim posted a Kindness Games shout-out that mentioned me. It was part of his overtime #8 segment, which was a joint call with Kathleen Fariss (known to many of us as Coach Kat). *Overtime* is anytime a TKG participant posted after their initial 30 days. I checked my cell phone and watched the entire TKG discussion between Tim and Kathleen. Toward the end of the post, Tim recognized me for my kindness.

I was blown away. I had been watching Lee and Tim's TKG journey, which had begun the month before. Tim, a corporate security "big wig" I had only met and interacted with a few times, had just publicly acknowledged me on LinkedIn, for the entire world to see, for being kind. But the thing was, once you were recognized in The Kindness Games, you were encouraged to join them. Once the shock wore off, all I could think was: Oh fudge! (Except it was not fudge.)

I do not have time for this, I thought. *I do not have 30 people to nominate. I do not know how to make or post videos for public consumption on LinkedIn. And oh, I really do not have time for this.*

I had a brief conversation with my wife about it. I showed her the video of Tim and Coach Kat. I explained all my reasons for why I couldn't do it, and she simply said, in her own loving way, "Okay." Nothing more, just, "Okay." Anyone in a loving relationship knows that any conversation that ended that way likely had much more to it.

I thought about everything going on then. The COVID-19 pandemic had most of the world in lockdown, social and civil unrest was near its peak following the death of George Floyd, and contested elections approached in the United States. Moments after that conversation with my wife, my resistance melted away and my mindset shifted.

I thought, *I will make time for this. I do have 30 people to nominate, and more, I will figure out how to make and post videos for public consumption on LinkedIn. And oh, I want to make time for this.* I knew this was an opportunity to spread kindness in a time when it was so dearly needed, and it was an opportunity to show my children what kindness truly looked like.

The Process

I made my first post that same night. One of my best friends had just been passed over for a very deserved promotion at work, and I felt that he was in need of a kindness shout-out. I waited until our younger kiddos went to bed to try that first video. I was tired after a long day at work, and I felt awkward in front of my laptop camera, but I was doing it.

For my second post, I took my laptop outside in the backyard for a beautiful Saturday morning in Northern

California. We have a swing set and slide in our backyard (for our younger children) that were visible in that video. Unbeknownst to me, my future TKG nickname would start right then and there: Playground Bill. The second video was admittedly easier, and I did not feel quite as awkward. I added some text at the beginning of my video in an attempt to be a little splashier, a little more like Brandon Tan's videos (read Brandon's story in Chapter 11). The process became easier over time, and I made sure that I set aside 30 minutes each day or night to craft a video and post on LinkedIn.

I started with a list of 30 people I planned to give shout-outs. The list did not change dramatically over those 30 days, but there were some substitutions and changes in order due to current life events. My Kindness Games shout-outs spanned from people I knew well to people I had only met virtually through LinkedIn — people with family members suffering from serious diseases, people who showed me the path to success, people who shattered glass ceilings long ago, people who have been teachers in subjects not ordinarily taught in school, and people who are no longer among the living in the form of legacy shout-outs.

While it's nearly impossible to choose my favorite posts, I wanted to highlight two strong female role models in my life who I acknowledged in my 30-day TKG journey. Ms. Betty Holden was my third-grade teacher. Ms. Holden was strong, passionate, and incredibly kind to everyone. I stayed in touch with Ms. Holden well into my late teens. Marylene Delbourg-Delphis founded a technology company in Silicon Valley in the late 1980s. I worked for Marylene and her startup for several years after high school, and I am still in awe of the glass ceilings she shattered so many years ago. Marylene was driven, a fantastic listener, and incredibly kind to everyone.

Both Ms. Holden and Marylene set the tone for my life in so many ways. They established that women can do anything men can — and many things men cannot — do, and that being kind is a key ingredient to success.

My Core Why

I don't spend much time thinking about whether I am kind or not, nor do I spend much time thinking about how I can be kind to others. I see kindness as an action, coupled with an opportunity. I'm finding that those opportunities can either be presented, or they can be created.

I have long believed in treating people with respect and kindness, and that culture has been affirmed by my life experiences. Being in law enforcement for over 25 years, I've seen the good, bad, and even worse, and many of the people I've encountered never wanted to cross paths with me. I believe in treating everyone like you would like and expect to be treated. Kindness, empathy, and respect go a long way in building relationships.

My "core why" has everything to do with family. I have three children, and I know all too well that children are always watching, learning, growing, and seeking out their own path through the paths they observe and experience. The Kindness Games quickly became a talking point in my family. We incorporated ideas I had learned from other TKG participants (thank you Sue Ginsburg — read her story in Chapter 9) into our Sunday family brunch meetings and other activities.

More importantly, I welcomed and encouraged our children to participate in The Kindness Games and many of my posts. I specifically shouted-out my father-in-law, Mark Phelps, early in my 30-day journey. I followed it up with a shout-out to our three children. And I finished the 30-day journey with a well-deserved shout-out to my incredible wife. Our kiddos not only appeared in that video, but they also crafted their own speeches about why they wanted to recognize their mom for her kindness.

Special Guest Contribution from Jenna Elise Massey (age 8)

This "guest" contribution from our eight-year-old daughter should show you the true impact The Kindness Games had and continues to have on our entire family.

The Kindness Games is something I think everyone should participate in. By watching my dad do it, I have learned that kindness is a very important thing. I actually helped my dad with a video for my mom.

I also think that love, care, and respect should be just as important. I hope that my dad and everybody else who participated in The Kindness Games will be just as kind to the people they work with, the people around them, and the people they live with. I hope that The Kindness Games continues, and that people will stay just as kind. It does not matter if you have no experience with The Kindness Games, just try to be kind to the people you may not even know. The Kindness Games is something that people should keep spreading with all the people they may not even know.

– Jenna Elise Massey

May 12, 2021

The Kindness Games *Alumni* (those who participated in TKG) have established a LinkedIn group message, as well as periodic gatherings over Zoom. I was promoted to our chief position at my job in late March 2021. To say the first two months of the new job "at the top" were unexpectedly rough would be an understatement. On the morning of May 12th, one of TKG Alumni Zoom calls was scheduled to take place. Those familiar feelings of "I don't have enough time. I have so much to do at work. I just can't. . ." all crept in that morning. But a calm voice inside me spoke up and simply said: "Okay." It was not my wife this time; it was me. A minute later, I realized logging into the TKG Alumni call was not simply something I should have done. Just like my decision to participate in The Kindness Games, I was making a conscious decision that I wanted to be part of the call.

I had met some TKG Alumni participants on that call before, at least virtually. There were a few participants I had not met, and we had a guest contributor as well: Rob McKenna, PhD, from WiLD Leaders. When it came time to do my virtual introduction, to my surprise, I started to share some of my recent work struggles. I let myself become vulnerable. I didn't go into great detail or talk for long, but it was incredible to see others' reactions to my vulnerability. As I was still talking, I began to receive private chat messages on Zoom from some of the other participants offering support and to talk more offline. Immediately after I finished talking, Rob McKenna spoke to me directly. He told me that I was in the middle of a storm, and what I just shared is exactly his "why" for what he does each and every day. When he recognizes someone is struggling, he reaches out to them. I watched nearly every participant lean in closer to their computers as they reached out to me.

Later that same day, into the next day and the week that followed, TKG Alumni reached out on a regular basis to check up on me — because that's what we do in The Kindness Games. I'm so grateful I was offered an opportunity to be part of an incredible support group whose mission is simply to care and to be kind.

Chapter 2:
Rediscovering Myself

by Heidi Tripp, PSP, Security Professional

Heidi Tripp is an experienced security professional with a passion for taking on new challenges in the workplace and beyond. She has seen firsthand the transformative power of compassion, empathy, and understanding. By sharing her experience, she hopes to inspire others to create a culture of kindness.

I read over the words one last time and thought, *I have to post this today, or I know I'll never commit to doing it.* I'd already delayed starting twice and wouldn't be able to complete the challenge. I had told people I was doing it, and I'd told myself I was doing it. But still I was questioning myself: What if nobody reads it? What if the person I wrote about gets embarrassed? What if I feel embarrassed? I'm not active on LinkedIn — what if nobody sees this? Maybe I should call a friend for a second opinion.

I'd been working at home for almost a year, which wasn't bringing out the best in me. I was really doing well until that week. It had been an entire year, and we'd missed out on so much. I did finally post what I wrote, and I ended up completing the challenge — eventually.

Unexpected Solitude

It hadn't been until we got the first stay-at-home orders that I realized how serious the COVID-19 pandemic really was. I was six months pregnant at the time, so excited to meet my daughter and become a mother. We'd been trying to get pregnant for almost three years, a painful experience that had already made me feel isolated. Most of my friends had young children, so they were always talking and connecting. Sometimes I felt invisible. It's tough when you feel like you can't relate to the people you love.

I'd had plans to go out to dinner with some girlfriends for my birthday, but that was the weekend that Rhode Island shut down restaurants, so we canceled it. I'd planned to attend ISC West and the ASIS Women in Security Leadership Summit, but those were canceled, too. My baby shower was canceled. My husband and I had even planned to take a short vacation a few months before the baby was born, but — you guessed it — canceled.

The news was overwhelming and filled with confusion over the virus. I started to tune it out. Nobody seemed to know how it was spreading or how we should protect ourselves. I felt inundated with COVID-19 confusion, press conferences, and dashboards with daily updates on the number of new infections and deaths.

Social norms and social codes were placed on pause while we tried to determine what the new rules were. We were all constantly engaging in awkward conversations as we tried to navigate one another's new comfort zones and boundaries. I didn't leave the house for months except to walk around the neighborhood and go to my doctor's appointments.

Claire was born in June. By then, the picture had become somewhat clearer. Everyone I knew was working from home. Most people weren't seeing friends or family. We were social, but only with a small group of friends, and even then, we wore masks and met outdoors. As the summer moved on, things began to feel more normal. We developed new routines and changed our habits, ordering everything online — even our groceries. I made friends with all the neighbors and socialized by walking around the neighborhood and beaches near my house. The warm summer months in New England meant that we could move around more freely; it was easy to spend time outside. With the addition of a new baby, our schedule likely would have changed anyway, and I lost sight of the fact that we were still in the midst of a pandemic.

I loved my summer with Claire, but as fall came, I was excited to return to work. I missed my job, my colleagues, and my customers. I was also looking forward to a little more structure in my day. I yearned for an atmosphere of growth, and I was eager to get back. I returned to work with all the enthusiasm of a kid returning to school in the fall. I even bought a new fall wardrobe — online, of course. But having spent the summer at home, I had forgotten that the job I was returning to was entirely different from the one I had left. Most of my colleagues were working remotely. Most of my customers were not taking in-person meetings. Just like our everyday routines at home had changed, there were new priorities in the workplace as a result of COVID-19. And there was still a lot of uncertainty.

Needless to say, work wasn't everything I'd hoped. My work style was seriously challenged. I felt like everyone else was already going full steam ahead on this new journey, and I was still trying to get started. I was uncomfortable with the new virtual work environment. I didn't feel seen or heard. I was unsure of how to engage, and I didn't feel proficient at messaging people online or talking to them in video calls.

I'm beyond extroverted. I thrive around people. I've always felt comfortable walking into any room, and I do it with confidence. I enjoy walking down a busy city street, eating in a crowded restaurant, and moving through the hustle and bustle of airports and coffee shops. I love the idea that I never know what might happen or who I might meet.

But sitting behind my computer screen was another story. Digital networking and virtual meetings were completely outside of my comfort zone, and it shook my confidence to the core. This feeling of insecurity felt new but also familiar. It was a feeling of powerlessness, of not having a say. I didn't have control over the world or my work environment. I felt as though the things that had made me successful in the past had all been stripped away from me. I was completely exposed. I needed to find a way to reconnect with people, fast.

I wanted to return to a growth mindset. I needed to move forward in my career. I needed to change the way I worked. That's when I hatched the plan.

The Plan

If you've known me for more than five minutes, you know that I love goals and goal setting. I'm always trying to do a little better today than yesterday. I love the idea of fresh starts, clean slates, and resolutions. I figure out where I'm going and what it's going to take to get there. So, I conquered the problem the only way I knew how: by backing up and asking myself, what are my priorities?

The virtual work environment created by the pandemic meant that my job had completely changed, and I felt left out of the conversation. I wanted to get comfortable working in this new virtual world. I had lost my ability to connect and network, and I needed to find a way to make that part of my normal day-to-day activities. I also needed to become more comfortable expressing myself through writing — something that was particularly tough for me, since it's not my preferred method of communication. I'm not always sure my writing conveys what I'm trying to say, and it's far from effortless. I've always been concerned about how my writing could be perceived. So much is communicated though nonverbal communication, and that's lost when written communication is the standard.

I first became aware of The Kindness Games when my colleague Kelsey Carnell took on the challenge. At first, I thought it was just a sweet idea — that she was brave to take it on, but it definitely wasn't the sort of thing I would do. I've always felt a little guarded online. I think I'm nostalgic for a time when people interacted with each other in person, and we didn't walk around with computers in our pockets. In recent years, I started to think, I'd like to be better at managing an online persona, but how would I get started? Since I wasn't active on social media, I always thought if I did post something, it needed to be significant. To join The Kindness Games, I'd need to use LinkedIn more and begin posting on the platform.

We didn't know how long the pandemic would last or what the world will look like in the future. I had to pivot, and I realized that The Kindness Games would give me a way to do it. It could be both a resolution and a way to get me where I wanted to go. I'd commit to 30 posts. It would create activity online. I'd become more comfortable with using LinkedIn as a platform, posting online, and communicating through writing. I'd stay true to my brand, reconnect with my network, and thank the people who'd influenced me and helped me get to where I am.

I made a list of almost 60 people, and next to each name wrote a characteristic or trait that person has that I admire, as well as how they'd impacted my personal life or career. I planned a schedule: 30 posts in 30 days. I would end on my birthday. I chose that timeline because it would be a countdown to the one-year mark of the initial shutdown. A bit grim, but it was a way for me to gain a little momentum at a time when I needed direction. The stage was set. There was nothing left to do but get started.

Chain Reaction

Over time, posting regularly made me comfortable with LinkedIn. It became easier and easier to write my posts, and I no longer fretted over them or what I would write. They got positive attention, so my network and my visibility grew. I had many friends and colleagues mention that they'd seen the posts. People were coming to my profile, sending me private messages, asking to join my network, and even asking me for advice.

The energy was contagious. Not only was I becoming more comfortable engaging on LinkedIn, but in virtual meetings and online chats as well. For me, The Kindness Games created a confidence snowball. Overcoming my fear of posting online led to eagerly taking on new challenges, even things I might not have considered before — for example, writing this piece for the anthology. New goals popped up out of nowhere. I no longer wondered what I was working toward; I was reenergized and eager to see what would come next.

The reaction to my posts surprised me. I expected people to respond, but some of the subjects of my posts seemed truly touched. Every single person replied on their post or in a text or call; most did both. Some posts seemed to resonate beyond the person. When I got it right, it was really right. I wasn't the only person who recognized their traits and qualities. The subjects of my kindness posts and the network of people around them recognized the person in my words.

I had been so worried about missing the mark or saying the wrong thing that I hadn't even considered the potential of getting it right. People seemed touched that the recognition was public. I'd been concerned that they might feel exposed or called out, but most seemed to feel that it meant more because it was shared in front of their colleagues and our industry. I was worried the posts would go out into the world and just sit there, but some of them took on a life of their own and continued to pop up and circle back around me for days or even weeks, giving me a little happiness jolt each time.

Facing my fear and overcoming it brought back my self-confidence and made me feel like myself again. I became reenergized and eager to see what would come next. Another thing I didn't expect to find when I started my posts was the community that existed around The Kindness Games or how welcomed and supported they would make me feel. They reach out every day —supporting each other, engaging with each other, and cheering on new members. The Kindness Games alumni built a growing support network and have expanded the mission to spread kindness every day.

Lessons Learned

As I'm writing this, Rhode Island has lifted the mask mandate. I'm planning Claire's first birthday party. Her grandparents are even planning to fly here from Georgia to celebrate. Work travel and in person meetings are back. My office has plans to return to work in the fall. Traffic may be worse than ever. The entire world changed overnight, and it's changing back almost as fast.

I can't recall another event in my lifetime that has touched everyone, everywhere. While we each have our own unique experience of living and working in the pandemic, the shared experience it created is undeniable. COVID-19 brought hardship, pain, and loss in different ways and degrees to all of us. Still, I believe some good has come out of this time.

I yearned for things to go back to "normal" — to travel, meet people in person, and socialize freely. Now I want to be intentional about how I live, work, and play, and with what I'm reintroducing back into my life. When I reflect on this time, I'll think about the people I've met and the role The Kindness Games played in renewing my confidence and bringing joy back into my life. I've learned a few things that I'll be bringing forward with me into the future.

It's about the Journey

The Kindness Games brought me back to a truth I've always believed but had lost sight of: it's about the journey, not the destination. You wouldn't set out on a vacation thinking about all the places you planned to visit, the sites to see, and the route to take, and then conclude that your final destination was home, so you needn't bother making the trip. Life is like that. Some places or times will be underwhelming, but others will take your breath away. In the end, it's often the things that go wrong that are the most memorable and make for the best stories.

Know Yourself

Reminding myself of what was important to me gave me the roadmap for how to move forward. When I found myself in uncomfortable and unfamiliar territory, it was difficult to know what to do next. I needed to embrace a new way of networking. This challenge gave me connection, allowed me to practice empathy, and was an opportunity for me to learn and grow beyond my comfort zone. The Kindness Games was a bridge back to myself because it was a project I could take on that would help me overcome my fears of networking virtually and posting online in a way that aligned with my core values.

Be Authentic

Working from home together has been a humanizing experience. It blurred the lines between our work lives and personal lives. We got to know our coworkers on a more intimate level. We had face to face conversations from our home offices, often in our living room, at the dining room table, or from a spare bedroom. Parents had to balance working with remote learning. Spouses, kids, and pets made surprise appearances on video conferences. We connected with people we didn't typically see or work with in person.

Working virtually allowed us to meet and connect with people from all over the world. I've heard more than one story of really close friendships or professional relationships developing between people who have never met in person. Everyone has become more forgiving of personal conflicts or an occasional rooster crowing in the background of your video call. By not compartmentalizing parts of ourselves, we built deeper, stronger connections which will endure.

Be Willing to Be Vulnerable

In her book *Daring Greatly*, Brené Brown describes vulnerability as "uncertainty, risk, and emotional exposure" — all things that, if you're like me, you'd probably rather avoid. Therein lies the rub, because Brown's research found that, "Vulnerability is the birthplace of love, belonging, joy, courage, empathy, and creativity." We're all striving towards these things. That's why I took on The Kindness Games challenge, and why it was such a worthwhile experience. The biggest emotional rewards only come when you're willing to sit with some emotional exposure and uncertainty.

We Learn by Doing

In Gretchen Rubin's book *The Happiness Project*, she lists her "Secrets of Adulthood," a lighthearted list of truths she claims to have "learned with some difficulty as I'd grown up." Gretchen's very first secret of adulthood is: "People don't notice your mistakes as much as you think."

I spent weeks crafting my list of people to reach out to throughout my Kindness Games challenge. I fretted over the words in my first post. On several occasions, I consulted a close friend about the person I wanted to recognize and what I hoped to say, concerned that I might somehow miss the mark or expose someone else online by saying something that would embarrass them or rub them the wrong way. On one occasion, I recorded a video more than 10 times before deciding never to post it.

In the end, these concerns were completely overblown. My comfort level evolved and posting got easier and easier. Some of my posts were better than others. Some might have missed the mark. But the experience was invaluable, and I wouldn't change it for anything.

Ask for Help

I am a big believer that we get further together. I have an accountability team. We're a small group, all in different stages of our lives and our careers. We have different goals but similar mindsets. We meet weekly for a half hour to share our goals, progress, and plans for the week. I find that structured accountability and positive reinforcement is helpful as I try to make progress toward my goals. Sharing my goals and my obstacles with others has allowed me to get better at giving and receiving feedback. It's also helpful to get an outside perspective. Often we can benefit from someone who's looking at our problem through a wider lens or from a different perspective.

Spend Out

Spread kindness wherever you can, embrace empathy, and give people the benefit of the doubt. The Kindness Games was my way of giving back to people in my life who have given so much to me. Sharing with people how they have helped you and what you admire about them feels risky, but it's often even more rewarding than you expect. A study by Amit Kumar and Nicholas Epley of The University of Chicago found that people overestimate the awkwardness of expressing gratitude or giving another person a compliment while underestimating the appreciation and happiness boost it will give to the recipient. Read more about their findings in the 2018 *Psychological Science* article "Undervaluing Gratitude: Expressers Misunderstand the Consequences of Showing Appreciation."

Chapter 3: Learning to Receive Kindness

by Sarah-Marie Baumgartner

Sarah-Marie Baumgartner is the mother of three amazing children that keep her on her toes. When she isn't with her kids, she's working in her role as pediatric home care nurse, a career she loves. Drawing from her warrior mindset as a mom, nurse, and cancer and domestic abuse survivor, she continues her fight by advocating for programs that help others on their healing journey.

You'd think that after 15 years in nursing, I'd have perfected kindness. Given the reputation of the nursing profession, that may have appeared true — and it's my belief that there are certain occupations where a greater-than-normal dose of kindness is needed to be successful. But have you ever felt like you were on autopilot?

The Promise I'd Made

Early in my nursing career, I made a vow to myself that I wouldn't become jaded like the older nurses I worked with. Some had been nurses for over 30 years, and it was like they were just going through the motions taking care of patients. I wanted to promise myself and my patients that I wouldn't become like that.

Some shifts made it hard to keep that promise, especially given what was going on in my home life. While I was tending to others and pouring so much care into them, I was enduring an abusive marriage at home. Some days my tank was so drained, it was difficult to truly show others the kindness they needed. Still, I went through the motions for appearances' sake, so no one knew what I was going through. The kindness I gave others was an armor of sorts — only worn to hide the shame of what was really happening and never truly authentic.

I'd originally been on a fast track for management, which was exciting and validating. But the more successful I became in my nursing career, the more abuse I endured at home. That juggling act was hardly sustainable, and in 2016, both my career and my marriage came crashing to an end. I finally left my abusive marriage and, for a time, nursing. The cost of hyperfunctioning for so long had just about completely consumed me. I had very little left that I could pour into others. I needed to heal, and I needed to be selfish about it. I needed to fill my own cup. So, healing and my kids became my priorities, and that meant a self-sacrificing job in public service had to be put on hold.

My healing started with Brené Brown's book *The Power of Vulnerability,* which served as a catalyst for self-discovery and encouragement to remove the armor I'd worn for so long. I rediscovered the promise I'd made in nursing — and how I needed to make that same promise to myself. I needed to live with my eyes and heart open to the wonders and possibilities that life had to offer. One of the biggest lessons I had to learn was not so much how to be kind, but how to receive kindness from others — because for a very long time, I'd believed I was undeserving of it.

Kindness Is Intentional

Learning to receive kindness taught me that kindness is intentional. Once I learned that lesson, the real magic began. I was able to connect with people on a level I never had before. Guilt and shame melted away. I believed I was deserving of kindness. I'd like to say I learned that lesson quickly, but it took some time. It's been six years since I started my healing journey.

I went back to nursing, but I quickly realized I needed to set boundaries. I needed to be mindful to maintain the values and beliefs I had developed and connected to again, like the belief that I could take care of others without running myself into the ground. To keep my promise to bring true authenticity to my career, I needed to be intentional with my time and my kindness.

It was that understanding which led me to pursue entrepreneurship. I created my own company — one where I could help other victims and survivors of domestic abuse but maintain a life outside work in which I was not sacrificing my family or my values. A company in which I could truly give kindness to others in a way that was rewarding for both them and me.

With this newfound goal, I realized I was going to have to network — something the introvert in me was reluctant to do. This led me to LinkedIn and eventually to The Kindness Games.

Discovering The Kindness Games

In January 2021, I started networking with intention, looking for like-minded individuals who were willing to be vulnerable, authentic, and uplifting, and who had a desire to do more than just make money. I was seeking out people who wanted to make an impact on the world. It didn't have to be some major project — in fact, it's my belief that the biggest changes happen with the smallest of ripples.

I started to network in the security industry. To most people, this sounds odd — a nurse interested in security? To me, the idea wasn't so far-fetched. Just look at Maslow's hierarchy of needs: safety and security fall near the very foundation of self-actualization and optimum health. I had been on safety teams in the hospital whose purpose was to ensure adverse events didn't happen to patients. For me it's a form of preventative medicine. In the company I'm forming, safety is of the utmost importance for victims and survivors of domestic abuse.

My network began to expand rather quickly, but with intention. I was selective of who I connected with and made sure to have a conversation with each person. There were countless hardships caused by COVID-19, but one of its benefits was learning that we could easily and meaningfully connect with people who lived hundreds, sometimes thousands, of miles away.

This led me to meeting Lee Oughton and Tim Wenzel, and I had enlightening and meaningful conversations with both of them. At the time, I didn't know they were the creators of The Kindness Games — in fact, I didn't even know they knew each other. As I networked with others they knew and began to see posts giving shout-outs to people who had made an impact in their lives, my curiosity piqued, and I started looking for the posts. What was this thing called The Kindness Games, and how could I get involved? I reached out to Tim for some answers.

Once I have a mission, I tend to be the kind of person who dives in headfirst, but I wanted this challenge to be different. Although the goal was 30 posts in 30 days, I wanted to take my time with it. I didn't want to become jaded by trying to get out 30 posts in 30 days. It's not that I think it's an unrealistic goal, but after six years of healing, I know myself better and have a deeper understanding of how I give and receive kindness.

Kindness is intentional. And so, my journey with The Kindness Games began.

Every Journey Begins with the First Step

Anyone who knows me will attest that I am type A on some things. So, when I decided to start posting, I researched how to do it first. I went through Lee's and Tim's LinkedIn profiles and watched a few of their videos to get some ideas. I would later learn that all the prep wasn't necessary; all I needed to do was be intentional and speak from the heart.

Nervous, I made my first shout-out post in May 2021. My first post on The Kindness Games journey was made to my Taekwondo family as I was getting ready to close out a chapter of my journey there and test for my black belt. Looking back, I remember my first steps on my Taekwondo journey, starting as a white belt and after five years of hard work and dedication, testing for my black belt. It felt fitting and timely that I would give my first shout-out to the very people that helped me accomplish that goal. They were there for me when I first left my abusive marriage and played a huge part in helping me gain back my confidence and trust in people. They welcomed me and my children with open arms.

Finding My Kindness Groove

I started struggling about halfway through my Kindness Games journey. The first posts flew by, and it felt wonderful to acknowledge those new connections I had made on LinkedIn. It seemed logical to give thanks to all the people who were taking time from their schedule to help me navigate this new world of entrepreneurship that I was embarking on. But as I made it quickly through the list of people I wanted to shout-out and give thanks, I found I needed to start digging a little deeper into the "why" of my posts. This is where I began to see how kindness is intentional. I took time to really sit and think about the person I wanted to shout-out. What were the personal touches they showed to me that affected me in a deeper way?

It was at this time I also realized I was just going through the motions of kindness in my nursing career. It was those times when I added a personal touch for my patients that I truly saw hope and healing occur. Armed with my newfound knowledge, I jumped back on the kindness trail and completed the last of my posts. Some posts were for specific people and others were for a community of people. The hardest posts to make were the ones for my mother and father. I lost my father in 2000 to melanoma skin cancer. My mother passed years later in 2012 of angiosarcoma. There was something cathartic about making a public declaration of how blessed and thankful I was for the time I had with them and their influence on my life.

The Kindness Games Alumni

Little did I know that when I completed my 30 posts, which for me took roughly three months, I would be inducted into a community of "Kindness Crusaders" as Lee so fondly calls us. The day I completed my last post, I was invited to join the alumni group thread.

Joining this thread was quite the surprise and one I am thankful for to this day. I was able to learn more deeply about other alumni kindness journeys. Beyond that, I learned more about their work and what they were doing in their communities, regions, and even on international levels. I had joined a collection of amazing people with the same mindset: that kindness heals in unimaginable ways. We banded together not only to continue our own shout-outs in something Lee and Tim dubbed overtime, but also to recruit and encourage new participants on their journeys to post 30 shout-outs.

I can genuinely say it is through The Kindness Games that I have met some of the most inspirational and supportive people. Whether someone is looking for a job change, or just needed some uplifting words, The Kindness Games alumni are there for each other. Over the past two years, I have had the pleasure of meeting some of them in person, and I look forward to the day I can meet them all. A big family reunion in which one thing stands out — kindness is intentional — and everyone there lives that by example.

KEY TAKEAWAYS

The Elephant in the Room: Vulnerability

1	**Make time for what matters to you.** Don't get hung up on what you "should" do. Make a conscious decision to do what's important to you. Otherwise you'll never find the time.
2	**Lean into the discomfort.** It can feel uncomfortable to be vulnerable, but feeling connected with and truly seen by others is worth the initial discomfort. It also gets easier the more you flex your vulnerability muscle.
3	**Get personal.** When recognizing others, go into detail about what you appreciate about them. Don't worry about getting too personal. Generally, people appreciate truly being *seen* by others.
4	**Kindness is intentional.** Being kind is a conscious choice. Consider how you can show kindness to others and to yourself.

The Curiosity Quest:
Seek Understanding

To be secure in our humanity, we seek to be known, to be loved, and to be accepted. These are the building blocks of belonging. People are people, no matter where you are in the world or where they're from. Customs and cultural norms will change and create interesting experiences, but people are the same. You can't understand or know someone by the way they look, where they're from, or how they talk. The outside never truly informs the inside, and the inside is so much more complicated and nuanced than we could ever guess. Even people who hold beliefs that we don't understand, disagree with, or even reject outright are people with a story, a rational and unique experience, and a journey which help make sense of their views, even if we can't understand the frame of mind ourselves.

Everyone desires to be known and that life is more interesting when we invest in learning about others. It's what makes dinner entertaining and worthwhile!

Being curious and open to engaging respectfully during meaningful conversations is paramount to understanding who someone is, what their experiences have been, and how these have shaped their perception and ideas about life. As individuals, we each have a single set of experiences, a single perspective on the world around us, a single philosophy on life. We challenge that by being curious about each other and by wanting to understand the journey of another and to hear about their experiences and ideas. Wanting to understand why they have certain thoughts, ideas, and opinions shows us that we are not 100 percent right about most things — we can't be. Our opinion of right often leads to wronging others if we don't practice empathy. It's impossible to have empathy when you can't even fathom a different perspective or idea.

Having meaningful conversations creates vulnerability. It creates a safe environment to open up about struggle. It opens the possibility that you may not know, you may not be right, and you may not understand. There's a strong possibility you will be asked about your beliefs. What will you say if they don't agree? What if they offer a counterpoint? What if they offer an alternative perspective? Begin with curiosity. You can choose to learn and ask questions. Choose to understand the human in front of you a bit more and admire the beauty and brokenness of their journey.

A common false choice is that you have to hold an opinion on everything. False choices are choices that imply that the universe falls neatly within an either/or scenario, and that no other choices exist. If you must have an opinion, then you must pass judgment on information as it crosses your awareness. If you have to hold fast to an opinion, it becomes difficult to listen to someone else's perspective without feeling insecure, arguing, and getting defensive.

The truth is you don't have to hold an opinion on everything. You can choose not to care about certain things. Or you can choose to learn, accumulate information, research information, and understand something new. Having knowledge that's contrary to your beliefs doesn't necessitate you change your beliefs. It provides you with a more diverse perspective on the topic. When you have meaningful conversations and learn another's perspective, you don't have to pass judgment. You don't have to fit this information into a belief system in the moment. You don't need to agree with them at all. . . Just learn and appreciate them, their journey, and their perspective.

When Lee first posted that we would be sharing videos for the next 30 days, I sat back in my hotel room and thought about whom I would choose to type up a small thought of gratitude. Who would qualify, why would they qualify, and what meaningful theme could this take on? The more I pondered my current state and how I had arrived at this very strange point in my life, the more I began to think about "The Hunger Games" movies. How we were being forced to attack and destroy assigned "enemies" who really hadn't done anything to us. It seemed to be a sport for the enjoyment of a few at the expense of the majority. For the first time in my life, I was hesitant to broach certain topics in conversation out of fear.

As I began my day, I noticed that I had a meeting with my friend Kehkashan Dadwani. I hadn't seen or spoken with her in six months, since we left the office. I excitedly jumped on the call and greeted my old friend. Happy to be catching up after so long, we exchanged the state of our new reality and how WFH (work from home) was going. Then I asked, "How are you dealing with all of this? Are you okay?" Kehkashan laid her burdens, frustrations, and anxieties on me because we were friends, and she knew she could do so without judgement. As she vented her frustrations and asked rhetorical questions, it became clear to me that over the previous two or three years, there were many things and opinions we had never discussed, because they weren't important. But now, those unimportant things were the basis of our current affairs, and it seemed that no friends survived if they existed on opposites sides of the aisle.

I didn't think any differently of my friend. In fact, I was honored with the confidence she had placed in me, but I was concerned that our friendship was going to end. The media, our politicians, our current world were telling us both that we had nothing in common with each other and furthermore, we couldn't be friends. As she shared, I wondered if sharing my views, letting her know that I don't agree with most of hers, would shatter our friendship. Was I willing to lose a friend over pettiness? Was I willing to silently nod and not share my feelings? Would I be willing to lie to maintain this friendship? Then it hit me, I could lead with curiosity and seek to understand our differences. I also trusted that she would appreciate the honesty and returned confidence. If I did this right, it should strengthen this friendship.

I asked Kehkashan if I could share a story with her. My wife and I were spending time with our neighbors and through our conversation, some political topics came up. I shared my opinion that some of what we hear in the media isn't the full story, and it seems that sometimes pertinent information is left out intentionally.

Our neighbors defensively asked if we were Republicans. They were surprised to find out we were conservatives and equated that with us being racist, homophobic bigots. I responded, "We have been acquainted for almost six months now. Have you felt threatened at all by us during this time? If we are in fact so dangerous, why are we spending the afternoon together right now?"

Kehkashan was silent and looked mildly shocked. I then asked her, "Have you ever felt threatened by me over the past three years, Kehkashan?" "No," she replied. I said, "Now that you know my views and that I most likely disagree with 90 percent of what you just shared with me, will we be able to remain friends?"

That 30-minute sync turned into 90 minutes and resulted in a series of 60-minute syncs each week going forward. My hope and conviction were true. We decided that our world was in a frenzy and our community fabric in tatters, and the only way to fix this was to be bold, to speak up respectfully, to lead with curiosity, and to be open to learning and knowing one another more deeply. We decided that we needed to invest in our friendship with honesty and to ground each other in this turbulent world and walk this journey together, so we could have a chance to heal our communities and change our world.

Kehkashan was my first Kindness Games shout-out. By opening up to Kehkashan with vulnerability and curiosity, we began to understand a different path. Instead of jumping to conclusions and quick judgements, we could approach our differences with empathy and kindness.

In This Section

As you read the following stories by Angela, Kelsey, and Kehkashan, consider how each of them is curious to understand others. Here are some of the major themes you'll find in their contributions.

Angela enjoys getting to know people beneath the surface and finds joy in sharing, "I know who you are, I know what you did for me, and I want to acknowledge you and your kindness." Kelsey leads with curiosity and poses the essential questions, "Why is it that when we're kids, we're so open to sharing things — toys, thoughts, and stories? Why are we so curious as kids and not as adults? Why can't we all continue to start with curiosity rather than judgement?" Kehkashan reflects on how being kind takes courage, especially with people who are different from us, who we disagree with, or who we just don't know.

Chapter 4: The Power of Transformative Questions

by Angela Scalpello, Owner and Principal of
The Scalpello Group, LLC

Angela Scalpello helps teams and organizations deliver on their objectives and become higher performing. She facilitates workshops on leadership, organizational culture, and Emotional IQ. Certified in the Four Rooms of Change and Conversational IQ, Angela helps enable individuals and organizations to successfully move through the stages of change and create trusting relationships and cultures that unlock co-creation, innovation, and transformation.

It's raining here in the Poconos. It's early morning, so everyone else is still asleep, but today is the deadline for me to write my piece about The Kindness Games. The only sound is the rain as it hits the roof in a steady and calming rhythm. It's not lost on me that I'm writing this the same way I did many of my Kindness Games posts — last minute and barely on deadline. So I'm telling myself the same thing I did then: "Angela, you made a commitment, so do it."

The Reluctant Participant

I hadn't thought about participating in The Kindness Games until Tim Wenzel approached me. Tim and I knew each other from some work we had done through Getting Security Done as well as with his team at Facebook. I'd been watching his TKG videos and seeing the responses they were getting not only from the people he was giving a shout-out to, but also those witnessing the outpouring of kindness, warmth, and inclusion.

Tim, along with Lee Oughton, had started The Kindness Games in September 2020. At the time, most of the world had been struggling with COVID-19 and its social, economic, and health impacts for more than six months. If there ever was a time to help ease social isolation and bring people together through stories of kindness and impact, this was it.

By the time Tim reeled me in with that initial video conversation, my coaching and team development consulting business — which had sputtered at the beginning of lockdown — was busier than ever. I, as well as my clients, had successfully navigated the pivot to virtual coaching, workshops, and team facilitation. How would I fit another task into my already full days? And yet, how could I not?

It wasn't just Tim's persuasive personality that had me asking myself that question (though it wasn't an insignificant factor); it was a question I had already started, and continue, to ask myself. The question is a compound one. It begins with, "What are you telling yourself you want, Angela?" followed by, "What are you actually doing?" I ask clients these questions often as they, for example, say they want a promotion, and yet never let anyone know about their accomplishments or ambitions. I gently ask friends these questions when they want to make a life change and yet struggle to change everyday habits that could contribute to it.

At the time Tim approached me, I was struggling with such sadness — about the polarization in this country, the harsh talk, the episodes of racial injustice, the blaming, and the anger. Although my family and I remained healthy and safe, wracked neither by financial nor health issues, I felt a sense of grief for all we had let go of — the companionship of shared in-person experiences, the ability to plan — as well as the constant anxiety of deciding what was or wasn't safe to do. In my daily life, I was doing what I could to stay connected with others: checking in on Zoom or writing and mailing a handwritten letter daily to friends, colleagues, or family. And yet there were days it all felt overwhelming, like I was scooping out the Atlantic Ocean with a measuring cup — and some days, using a strainer instead.

So when Tim asked me to join The Kindness Games, I did so reluctantly. It was a classic situation of telling myself I wanted to counteract all the harsh rhetoric in the world, and yet, what was I willing to do? How could I use my voice on a powerful and public platform to both celebrate and pay tribute to individuals or groups who had made an impact on me?

My journey was also inspired by being the recipient of a Kindness Games shout-out, specifically the shout-out by Lisa Oliveri. I consider Lisa a dear friend, and like many special people in my life, our friendship began serendipitously and unexpectedly. I had interviewed Lisa on the phone as part of a project I was doing for a client on whose advisory board she sat, and we'd continued the conversation over lunch when I was next in Washington, DC. Lisa is warm, engaging, generous, smart, and kind. She's curious about others and open to her own growth and development. I had started to informally mentor her, and in her Kindness Games post, she mentioned what she saw as the impact of our relationship. I felt so seen and recognized and appreciated. Just as importantly, I realized that through my postings as part of The Kindness Games, I might be able do the same for others.

And so, reader, I said yes.

The Journey Begins

When I lament that I have no real hobbies (I don't do crafts, collect stamps, knit, or crochet, for example), those who know me best say that my hobby is collecting people. They don't mean that in a creepy, stalker way, but rather in an "aren't people fascinating, and don't they all have unique stories and selves" kind of way. I'm curious to uncover who people are beneath the surface. At this point in my life, I'm blessed (and I use that word intentionally) with friendships spanning all over the world, with people similar to me and also vastly different than me in terms of life choices, careers, age, interests, and beliefs. Each one of these people has enriched me and my life. So the idea of choosing just 30 individuals to highlight in my 30 days of The Kindness Games was a challenge, not because I would be scrambling for names, but because I would have to leave a number of people out.

Some of the people I chose were individuals who not only impacted me but were creating an even greater impact through the work they were doing. I realized that talking about groups of people could be powerful. One of my posts was a shout-out to mentors everywhere, and another was to sponsors everywhere (people who had spent political capital to advance someone else's progress or career). I also — to some surprise — gave a shout-out to bad managers. I wanted to point out that even in difficult situations, such as having to suffer through a bad manager, there is learning to be had.

Almost immediately, my posts gathered traction and feedback. After a few days, people were letting me know on group industry Zoom calls or in emails that they were following my posts. A number of people made a point to tell me how reading my Kindness Games posts cheered them up. Everyone I mentioned in a post commented. I felt happier knowing that, in essence, I was telling people in my life, some of whom I had worked with more than 15 years ago, "I know who you are, I know what you did for me, and I want to acknowledge you and your kindness."

Realizing the Power of "What If?"

In November 2019, I attended the NationSwell Summit in New York. One of the speakers was Tom Tait, CEO at TAIT & Associates. Tom was first elected the Mayor of Anaheim in 2010. He ran on a platform of making Anaheim the City of Kindness. I remember he said that after he won, he worked with his team to consider issues the city was facing through the lens of kindness. For example, how would they handle the issue of homelessness if they addressed it by asking: "What would be the kind thing to do?" It had to be practical of course, but how could it be done with kindness?

The message resonated with me on a number of levels. As a certified Conversational Intelligence practitioner, I know that a transformational conversation always includes a question for which we have no answer. Often the most powerful questions start with "What if?" What if we could work together, what would be the one thing we might do? What if we could find common ground, where might we start? I facilitated an entire post-acquisition team integration workshop by asking the group, "What if we wanted to create a community and culture of belonging, what would we do?"

I highlighted Tom Tait in Episode 14 of my TKG posts. What Tom had started in Anaheim, I realized Tim and Lee, and all my colleagues in The Kindness Games, were trying to spread around the world. What if we could educate our children to be kind to each other? Wouldn't they think twice before bullying or excluding another kid in the playground? What if we could look at our neighbors and think about what treating them with kindness would look like? If we were driving somewhere and saw someone trying to merge into our lane, what would be the kind thing to do? If we were in a meeting dealing with differences in opinion, rather than criticize, judge, or shut down, what would be the kind way to talk through and deal with the conflict?

There were many evenings during my 30 days of posting for The Kindness Games when I had to force myself to write a post, honoring my commitment to the team and the cause. After I'd written and posted my content, I inevitably felt better. I knew someone would see their name and my acknowledgment. Who knew when and how it would hit them? Would it come on a day they were questioning their own value and worth? Would it come following a disappointment? Some of the people I wrote about told me that my "timing was impeccable," as they had been in a challenging or sad place when my post appeared.

Looking back now, I realize that I need and want to continue these posts in some way. I want to spread the word about the power of kindness, of recognizing in a public forum how others have helped you, and to encourage others to think about doing the same. Maybe it will take a different form.

I remember when I got ready to post my first group shout-out. It was my 16th post, and it was to mentors everywhere. I wanted to celebrate all the people in the world who had helped someone through their support, advice, and caring, honest feedback. I wanted to thank people in my life who had believed in me, who had listened deeply and lovingly and, in doing so, had helped me grow. However, I wasn't sure if I was violating some "rule" of The Kindness

Games. Maybe there was a rule about only mentioning individuals? In fact, where were the rules of The Kindness Games? Had I overlooked them? Who could I ask about the rules? (On a side note, I sometimes say about myself: "You can take the girl out of the Catholic School, but you can't take the Catholic School out of the girl.") When I finally tracked down my answer about the rules of The Kindness Games, it was simply this: "The only rule of The Kindness Games is to be kind." How breathtakingly beautiful and simple it is in its clarity.

Thoughts for Reflection

I want to close by sharing a few things upon which you might reflect. They might spark opportunities for you to thank someone for the kindness they have shown you.

Even Small Things Have Impact – Look for Them

Sometimes when something comes easy to someone, they think it's something others can also easily do — so they often diminish both its value and impact. For example, a person for whom listening well comes naturally — in a deep way, to both connect and understand — might not realize how rare and valuable a gift that is. Letting the listener know what a difference it made to you being listened to, heard, and understood might come as a pleasant and gratifying surprise.

Remember Those Who Did the Work before You

All of us stand on the shoulders of others. All of us walk paths that, although not yet smooth, are less strewn with obstacles because of the toil and struggles of others. Let those earlier pathfinders know you're aware of what their earlier efforts have enabled.

There Are Many Opportunities to Choose Kindness

We are always called to make choices. We can choose how we speak, the words we select, and the tone we use in saying those words. When has someone made a choice that helped you? When you made a mistake, did someone choose not to yell at or shame you, but rather to turn it into a learning opportunity? Celebrate that person and that choice.

Kindness Is Never the Wrong Approach

We regularly hear the phrase, "Meet the person where they are." Yet we often don't know exactly where the person is in terms of their financial situation, family stressors, health status, or emotional challenges. In situations where the current stay of play isn't clear, choose kindness. It might not be exactly the "right" response, but it's never the wrong one.

Being Kind to Yourself Feeds Your Ability to Spread Kindness

And finally, show a little kindness to yourself. Self-kindness increases our capacity to be present and kind with others. Kindness is not a thing that's "nice to have" — increasingly, we're seeing it as a "must have."

I heard someone say about the pandemic that although we've all been in different boats, we've been in the same storm. In our lives there will always be storms, some larger and more turbulent than others. For ourselves and others, kindness can be that safe harbor in the storm and the promise that we will get through it together.

Chapter 5: Asking Questions to Understand

by Kelsey Carnell

Kelsey Carnell is an experienced young security leader and co-founder of The Kindness Games. She has a passion for people, helping others, spreading kindness and authenticity, thinking outside the box, and mentorship. Kelsey always challenges others to step out of their comfort zone and be curious enough to learn and grow from each interaction. Over seven years in the security industry, Kelsey has led volunteer groups, inspired others to drive change, connected with many, and helped lead annual sales growth.

When I first met Tim Wenzel in 2019, I didn't expect that our acquaintanceship would turn into a close friendship, mentorship, and eventually lead to a small global movement during the COVID-19 pandemic. I was attending the inaugural AcceleRISE — a young professionals conference organized by the Security Industry Association — and I saw this guy sitting at the back of the room. I recognized him as one of the speakers but wasn't sure if I had met him before. He looked so familiar. I walked up to him and asked, "Hey, do we know each other?" Tim looked up, smirked, and said, "No, I don't think so." I introduced myself, and over the rest of 2019, Tim and I began speaking regularly about everything: security industry questions, leadership tips, just catching up, and chats about our mutual love of Jeeps.

Stigma in the Security Industry

Tim and I first started truly working together when we both got involved with GSD (Getting Security Done), an industry thought leadership group that works to encourage positive leadership, forward progression, and change within the security industry. As we got to know each other better, we realized that we have a lot in common. Every time we talked, we got into deep, thought-provoking conversations about work and life.

During one of our first sessions, I started out by picking Tim's brain on the security industry's stigma towards young people and young women in particular. People tend to say things like: "You know this is a male-dominated industry," or, "You could be my grandchild, you're so young — what, did you just graduate high school?" I don't know if people who say things like this are aware of the perception they are giving to new, excited young professionals. Do they think they're somehow giving us advice? It might be easy for some people to brush these comments off or not think anything of them, but Tim and I wanted to do something to change the perception and potential adversity that others are facing into something actionable.

This was the start of our kindness journey. We wanted to overcome potential bias with curiosity and kindness. So, in true thought leadership fashion, we wrote an article together called "Curiosity Overcome Bias" in September

2020. We drew correlations between how isolated everyone was at the height of the pandemic and how quick they were to share an opinion without considering other views of a situation. We were all being blinded by bias. How could we make a positive impact in changing this disconnected mess we were facing?

Tim Lays Down the Gauntlet

On a dreary spring day in September 2020, I was doing my daily scroll through LinkedIn when I noticed that I'd been tagged in a post by Tim. He was giving me a shout-out for being a passionate and driven young security professional. I was taken aback by his kind words and intrigued by what he called The Kindness Games challenge. At the end of the video, he challenged everyone to join the games — anyone who wanted to "give a damn about others and recognize those that helped us get to where we are."

That was all it took. I've always been very intentional and open about thanking those who have helped me along life's journey. Three days later, I was getting ready for my cousin's graduation party. It was my first true outing in over a month. I'm a very social person and at this point during the pandemic, I was so tired of being stuck at home, working from home, wearing athleisure, and not having plans. As I got ready, you'd have thought I was going to prom! I took a minute to get out my iPad and make a list of 30 people to recognize, but 30 quickly turned into 85. I scribbled down a few talking points and pressed record. After many cuss words and aggravation because I couldn't nail what I wanted to say in a concise manner, I completed my first video shout-out in 15 takes — I wish I was kidding. That first shout-out went to my family, the four people who have had my back since day one who will inspire, motivate, support, and love me all the days of my life. It was game on from there!

Why Was This So Hard?

I've always been an extroverted person. I could talk to a wall. I thrive in networking opportunities, and I always seem to end up talking to the quieter people because I want everyone to feel like they have a seat at the table. Vulnerability isn't easy when you don't always know your audience, and speaking in a virtual atmosphere is tough. Posting a video on any social platform, especially LinkedIn, means your future employer, current boss, industry competition, etc., might see it.

As I got more comfortable recording, I started to make each shout-out more creative. I was no longer dressing up. I recorded while I was out for walks, sweating from my run, or sitting with the pup. I realized that people truly want to see the real, authentic you, not just the girl dressed up and ready for a party, especially during a time like the pandemic.

I felt reenergized by the shout-outs and feedback I was receiving each day. But I was shocked when I started receiving some pushback. People told me I was too happy, too passionate, or fake. I didn't understand why they were saying things like that. I thought I was being vulnerable, authentic, and passionate about others. In doing TKG, I was hoping to inspire others, put a smile on their faces, and help them step out of their comfort zone. How could people be so hateful?

There will always be people trying to bring down the good, but we are the captains of our own ships, and we are in charge of sailing, not them. Keep that fire burning, and don't let anyone dull your flame.

Leading with Curiosity and Kindness

Why is it that when we're kids, we're so open to sharing things — toys, thoughts, and stories? Why are we so curious as kids and not as adults? Why can't we all continue to start with curiosity rather than judgement? These are all questions I ask myself today. What if we all cared about each other, and took the time to ask questions to understand someone's perspective and story a little more before jumping to conclusions about them? We can't go into every conversation as if it's an argument and not a discussion. These questions are so important, and in the chaos of daily life, sometimes they fade. It's important to challenge yourself to do better. We always can do better, be better, learn, and grow. Never become complacent.

As Tim, Lee, Kehkashan, and I became the de facto "Kindness Committee" as the strongest proponents of TKG, we began to have more conversations about how to impact our work and live out the lessons of TKG day to day. The concept of Leading with Kindness was born, built upon the simple idea that if we lead with curiosity, it enables self-control in the face of adversity or stress. Curiosity leads to learning and wanting to understand the human on the other side of each life situation we're involved in.

Greatness comes from outside of your comfort zone. It's scary at times, but what challenges you allows you to grow. By being more curious, we can manage conflict better, approach relationships new and old with a more open mind and stay open to other points of view. Asking yourself why someone responded the way they did or asking them to help you understand opens a dialog for you to learn, listen, and grow from each and every human interaction.

Remember, we are in control of how we act and show up. Let's work toward getting back to a place where we can ask questions and learn from each other, rather than being so quick to judge.

Tips for "One-Take" Videos

- Make it short and sweet — be concise.

- Write down four bullet points on a Post-it note and place it right by your camera while recording. This will help you stay on track and hit the "high points."

- Be authentic — be proud to be you!

- If you mess up, that's life. People know that mistakes happen. Keep rolling!

- Outside your comfort zone is where greatness happens!

Chapter 6: Being Kind Takes Courage

by Kehkashan Dadwani, MA

"Resilience Rockstar" Kehkashan Dadwani is passionate about increasing awareness on the importance of mental well-being, especially in the security industry, and leading with heart and a growth mindset. She has managed successful programs, strategic partnerships, and business initiatives. She's well known for developing and launching scalable solutions to drive impactful outcomes for customers and companies through cross-functional collaboration and data-driven storytelling.

Being kind to those you love is easy. Yes, some days our patience is tested, but for the most part, our desire to be kind comes from a place of familiarity and safety. But what about being kind to those we don't know or don't agree with? It's easier not to think about it than to consciously be kind to people like that. Kindness, I've come to realize, takes courage — much like every great thing I've ever encountered in life.

On an early morning in 2018, when I would have typically gone straight into the micro kitchen at work to grab a basic cup of coffee, I instead decided to change things up. I ended up in a different building, craving a Philz Coffee, and as the aroma of the coffee shop hit me, I knew I'd made the right decision to go out of my way. While waiting for my coffee, I noticed a colleague I'd known in passing for a while waiting for his own cup of Philz. He didn't look like a morning person, and I almost left him to his thoughts. But today I was in rare form. I had deviated from my routine; who was I to question my impulse to network?

You have to understand, to those who know me, I'm the kind of person who can strike up a conversation with strangers and talk about anything or nothing at all. But that's just what people see from the outside — they don't see the panic or fear of rejection raging inside. That day, though, I didn't let my fear get the better of me.

"Hey, Tim! Long time, no see. How are you doing?" Those infamous words would become the prelude to my Kindness Games journey.

Knowing that kindness takes courage, and so does creating a community, I pushed past another fear and asked Tim if he had a few minutes to chat. He stared at me with those tired eyes desperate for caffeine, but still, he said: "Sure — let me grab my coffee."

That day, I gained an incredible friend and mentor in Tim Wenzel.

A Trip down Memory Lane

I've often heard there are moments in our lives that have the potential to change who we are. But there's a fine line between being impacted by a major life experience and letting it completely define you. For a long time, I thought of myself as a victim of circumstances — not realizing that in the end, what mattered most was my own mindset. How we think about ourselves, our existence, and what we stand for is equally as important for our happiness as having a fulfilling life.

I've learned that the best experiences in life and opportunities for growth come from a desire to learn, embracing the "suck," and seeing adversity more as a challenge than a roadblock. Yes, life hasn't been the easiest, but I've also had wonderful experiences beyond anything I could have imagined in adolescence.

My family landed in Houston, Texas, in the evening on August 11, 1999. We'd been traveling for 32 hours across multiple flights and layovers. We didn't know how to speak English. When we deboarded the plane, the heat and humidity in Houston reminded me of home — a place I would never call home again.

Just a few days before, my family and I had left most of our belongings and our remaining family in Pakistan to immigrate to the United States. We had the typical immigrant story — Dad came to the US with $50 to his name and worked himself to bits to provide for his family. We were in search of the American dream and a better life, and like most immigrant families, this would've been enough for us and provided our family a good life. But one of my first memories of being in the US is filled with confusion, terror, and pain.

It was my first day of middle school. I was told I was lucky because the school year had just started. I kept to myself, unnerved by the stares and whispers. During my final class, a teacher held me back to have a private conversation, and it was just long enough for me to miss the school bus. Luckily, my cousin had stuck around to make sure I didn't get lost. We called our parents to come pick us up, but after several hours, they still hadn't arrived. I felt angry and irritated. How could my mother abandon me in this strange place when I didn't even want to be here? Eventually, my mother's youngest sister came to pick us up. She didn't say anything, but just carted us into the vehicle and took us home.

My mother, one of her younger sisters, and my youngest sister had left to pick us up, but they never made it to the school because their car had been destroyed by an 18-wheeler. Both my mother and aunt were in critical condition. Somehow my youngest sister, who was in the back seat, had walked away without a scratch.

They say what doesn't kill you makes you stronger. I wish they told you how much the "what doesn't kill you" part hurts. How much healing it can take. I am stronger today because of what I experienced at the age of 11, and my mother and aunt are warriors because of what they survived. But it still doesn't make it easier.

Growing up in a small town in Texas was no easy feat. With little knowledge of English, I spent many years in ESL classes. I didn't know the word for it then, but what I really needed was an advocate. With my mother recovering from her injuries and my father working 12-plus-hour days to support our family, my sisters and I had to learn to advocate for ourselves.

As a freshman, almost a year after the September 11 attacks, I was still finding my way through American society and high school in particular. At my oldest sister's encouragement, I joined a journalism class to find someone who could help me master the English language. On the first day of class, as I walked into a room filled with American kids sharing their middle school newspaper accomplishments and aspirations to become professional journalists when they grew up, I felt absolute terror. I didn't belong. How could someone who could barely read, write, or speak the language do anything in journalism?

I found a mentor in the journalism teacher, Kerri Hays. She not only taught me the basics of journalism, but she also taught me to not be afraid of the English language. She gave me opportunities I couldn't have imagined before. I joined both the high school newspaper and broadcast staff, which eventually gave me the opportunity to join the Houston Chronicle in 2008 and complete an internship at Deutsche Welle in 2013. Kerri made it possible for a young immigrant to believe in her ability to pursue a career that both terrified and excited her.

Immigrating to the US was one of the best decisions my parents could have made. It gave me opportunities to advance as an individual. I am here today because of the sacrifices they made, but every dream comes at a cost. The cost of my American Dream was frequent adversity, hardship, and a constant questioning of my identity and what I "deserved."

Early in my youth, even before we immigrated to the US, I had dreams of achieving something great — I wanted to help society and leave my mark on this planet. I was different from my family and the kids I met in school. I always repeated a mantra in my mind: "If I shoot for the stars, I'll land somewhere close."

Adapting and Adjusting through Challenges

One of the greatest lessons I've learned is that working through adversity makes you stronger. And the best way to work through challenges is to adapt and adjust to the environment in which you find yourself.

With a global pandemic wreaking havoc on our plans and everything we'd hoped to accomplish that year, 2020 was a hard year for all of us. I was going through a lot of changes. I was living in San Francisco, California, when the pandemic started. In January 2020, I got engaged to my partner, who lived in Texas. When the pandemic started, thinking it would all be over in a few weeks, I packed a bag and flew from California to Texas to ride out the quarantine period with my future husband, using it as an opportunity to spend more time with him.

A few weeks turned into a few months, and eventually living out of a single bag got really old. In June 2020, I flew back to California to terminate my lease, sell everything I could, and moved everything else back across the country to Texas. If you've ever moved cross-country, you know how much of a pain it is. Doing it during a pandemic felt all that much worse. But I had to look on the bright side. I was getting an opportunity to spend more time with my partner than I had imagined I would get to when we got engaged.

When the pandemic started, it felt like we were all in it together. We all quarantined and made sacrifices so we could keep our communities safe. As the year progressed, the sacrifices being made by different communities changed. Our first responders stood on the front lines to protect us from ourselves. Different communities suffered from a lack of resources. We saw a rise in domestic violence because victims were forced to quarantine with their abusers, without a break, and there was limited access to shelters. We saw different communities spread hate against one another in an ever-more polarized world.

In September 2020, Tim and Lee launched The Kindness Games as a way to spread kindness and gratitude. Their videos were infectious. You couldn't help but join in and spread kindness. Joining The Kindness Games changed my life. It was a challenging year, but because of the community I joined, the pandemic had a silver lining. We all faced the challenges together and adapted to our environment. Tim and I started a podcast called "The Real Kindness Games," which helps shed light on our personal biases and encourages kindness by modeling curiosity in conversation. I met more people than I would've under normal circumstances, and my life is richer for it today.

Adversity and challenges come in all shapes and forms. Our ability to adapt to these situations and how we choose to look at them affect the outcomes and what we learn from the experiences. At the end of the day, we all have a choice: We can choose to be a victim of circumstances, or we can rise up and turn a challenge into an opportunity.

It's Just the Beginning

I am fortunate. I'm surrounded by an incredible community made up of my family, friends, mentors, colleagues, and network. I have found great success in my career not only because of what I invested in myself through hard work, determination, and adaptability, but also because of what others invested in me.

No matter what life throws at me, I look at life through a lens of positivity and kindness. There have been moments of darkness when I felt like all hope was lost. Depression, anxiety, and loneliness are unwelcome roommates, but with the help of my community, and seeking support and guidance from medical professionals, I have been able to build a fulfilling life that's meaningful and full of wonder. While early in my life I lacked mentors and advocates in my corner, I now have a rich community of them who surround and support me.

The Kindness Games started as a means to connect with our community and spread gratitude for those who had an impact in our lives, but it has become something so much more. How we live our lives and how we treat others is up to us. You can't be forced to join in the kindness journey. It's a choice you must make for yourself. Are you ready to join The Kindness Games?

KEY TAKEAWAYS

The Curiosity Quest: Seek Understanding

1

Learn to pursue curiosity.
We elevate others by learning about them and showing interest. When you're confronted with difference, pursue curiosity instead of judgement.

2

Curiosity helps us overcome bias and maintain self control.
It allows us to ask questions, gain information of another's perspective, and discuss instead of reacting. We can breathe, remain calm, and logically examine the issue at hand.

3

Be curious about yourself.
Challenge your preconceptions about yourself. Be curious about your why. Don't let shame or judgement cloud your understanding of yourself.

Wait, What the Fun?

As I made my list of people, I reflected on people who had been there for me during difficult times, people who had sacrificed with and for me, and people who have picked me up or invested in me. I found names and memories flooding my mind during my workday. Gratitude began to infect my thoughts and interrupt my workdays. My outlook improved, and the more I spoke life and truth to other people, the more I wanted to continue doing so. I began to crave sharing kindness. I had always thought of myself as a kind person, but how could I intentionally approach every aspect of my life with kindness? How could I intentionally build kindness and gratitude into my daily routine and individual interactions?

It didn't take long for people to jump in. Kelsey Carnell, Jason Sikora, Brandon Tan, and Josh Ladesma all jumped in early. But then something strange happened, people I didn't know began to join The Kindness Games. Within a few short months, we had participants from the United States, Mexico, Canada, India, and countries in Europe and Africa.

I didn't think The Kindness Games would catch on in a meaningful way, but suddenly I was meeting new, fantastic people. We all came together around the idea of spreading kindness. I found another curiosity — most of these people became close friends very quickly. The normal boundaries of unfamiliarity were absent. The feeling-out process to gauge the safety of a relationship shortened to mere minutes. A 30- to 60-minute Zoom call to meet a new Kindness Games participant would begin with introductions and background and somehow quickly move into the meaningful life topics: struggles, wins, hopes, and fears all shared in minutes. Most of these first meetings ended with recording a joint kindness shout-out.

People began to bring up posts they had seen in conversation — people who I never called out. People who had never liked, commented, or shared. It was bizarre to me how many people were consuming my content on a regular basis. I would have work calls with offices in Asia, Latin America, and Europe, and people would talk about their favorite posts and shout-outs. I was perplexed. So many people were passively consuming this content. When I asked them why they watched, they told me because it made them happy, it was funny, or it made them grateful for similar people in their lives.

Kindness as a Cure

November is a tough month. Thanksgiving is the beginning of the holiday season, and you basically have to wrap up your entire professional year at work by the second week of December before everyone checks out until the New Year. You get to work finalizing budgets, wrapping up projects, preparing for almost everyone being out of the office and offline, and solidifying the performance, goals, and achievements of your teams and programs for the annual report.

Coming into November 2020 I had what felt like a mountain of work. I also had a lot of extra activity in my personal life. My father-in-law's health continued to decline. He was spending more and more time in the hospital, six hours away, which meant my mother-in-law was with him, which meant the house and the kids left at home were kind of on their own. On the bright side two of the boys were old enough to look after the younger one, but cleaning and maintaining a household is not the strong suit of adolescent boys. We were also beginning to see the writing on the wall. Hospice was making daily visits to the hospital and helping them make arrangements for my father-in-law's discharge, where he would come home to be kept comfortable until he passed. My mother-in-law made arrangements from the hospital, and my wife needed to follow through with them at the house. Due to COVID-19 restrictions, we couldn't visit him in the hospital. My mother-in-law couldn't leave because she was his power of attorney, and the hospital only allowed one visitor to be registered per 24 hours, so if someone else visited, she wouldn't be available to make decisions should the need arise. On top of all of that, Thanksgiving was on the way, so my wife was picking up the tasks her mother would normally do. So, life was busy.

The second week of November, we received a call. My wife's last living grandparent had died. Her mother couldn't leave the hospital to plan or attend her own father's funeral. What a terrible burden she was under. My wife and I picked up the slack with the funeral planning. We spent every evening with her brothers to get them ready for the funeral while getting the house ready for their dying father to come home from the hospital. Her youngest brother began to sleep over at night. He needed the comfort and stability of a parental figure. We pulled it off. The visitation and funeral happened. My wife Zoomed the funeral, so her mother and other elderly family members who couldn't make it could attend virtually.

As soon as the funeral services ended, the schedule for my father-in-law's discharge from the hospital was set. He came home on Wednesday the week before Thanksgiving, and we were shocked when the ambulance delivered him. The whole family was in the house as they brought him in, and what we saw drove us all to tears. We couldn't believe our eyes. During the two months he had been in the hospital he had changed so much. He was in pain and very confused. He babbled as if he suffered from memory loss and communication problems, yet he was only in his 60s. The pain, medication, and his failing body had left him a shadow of who we remembered.

They moved him into his hospital bed, and his wife began to explain that he was at home. After five minutes he understood. He understood that he was home to die, and he began to cry. My wife and I were the first to talk to him, and everyone else followed suit. When he saw us, he knew who we were and had meaningful thoughts to share and questions to ask. After the family had cycled through, some of us went back to hang out near his bed and talk about whatever he wanted. After a couple hours he told us he was tired and needed to sleep.

He never woke up. He slept all day Thursday. We all gathered Thursday evening again. We spoke to him, played worship music nearby, and had conversations by his bed that we knew he would enjoy. Even though he didn't interact, he would sometimes groan or move when something was said or someone asked him a question. He would tap his fingers to the music and squeeze our hands. By 11 pm, we decided to go home, but before we could get to bed, the phone rang. Around 1 am on Friday, November 20th, my last father died.

Three years before, when my father died, it was sudden and a shock. He began having chest pain in the afternoon and was dead before evening. This was different — a long, drawn-out, painful process. As strange as it sounds, we were all relieved when it was finally over.

The Sunday before Thanksgiving we had his funeral. He was buried on Monday. Then on Tuesday, everyone continued showing up to be together. Thanksgiving was only days away, and it was difficult to be thankful. However, we stuck together and had a good Thanksgiving weekend, enjoyed the family time, and were about to enter December.

As I looked through my to do list for work, I had lost motivation. I couldn't concentrate, I didn't have the energy or drive to finish the year. My boss was very understanding. He gave me anything I needed, but he couldn't help me. Someone asked me, "Can you believe Christmas is only 30 days away?" Then it dawned on me, I have exactly 30 days to get to *triple overtime,* or 3OT. It was another 30-day increment of time, an opportunity to right my mental state and get back on track. I was on OT27, so if I could do 33 more posts, that would get me to triple overtime and hopefully lift my spirits and provide some motivation. I told the Kindness Committee about it, and we decided to call it the Jingle Bell Kindness, knocking out 30 posts in the 30 days between Thanksgiving and New Years. Several others on the Kindness Committee hopped on the bandwagon.

Similar to quarantine, this exercise fed me with mental positivity. Not only was I happier, but I was able to dig up the motivation needed to close out the year. Also, it got me planning. I realized that 2021 was going to be more of the same, but there would also be some curve balls. I had to figure out a healthier routine, organize my schedule and calendar to work for me and not bog me down, remain agile and productive, and not let the meetings build up to the point where I couldn't do the work. Jingle Bell Kindness gave me the perspective I needed to focus on positive changes to set me up for success in 2021.

I began to communicate clear instructions to my team at work on what I expected from each of them to ensure we all found work-life balance and intentionally maintained a healthy mental state. Self-care became our first priority in 2021 for everyone working with me.

Through participating in overtime, I reconnected with my support system during a really difficult time in my life. I even managed to have fun. When we are struggling with loss or other life difficulties, we revert to isolation. We put our walls up to protect ourselves. This is exactly what not to do, because it doesn't help.

In This Section

If you remain open to kindness, vulnerability, and connecting with others, fun and enjoyment will enter your life in ways you didn't expect. In the following stories, notice how Christopher, Michael, and Sue surprise themselves by having fun and how it affected their wellbeing.

Chapter 7: Be the Light

by Christopher Stitt

Christopher Stitt served more than two decades in leadership positions in federal law enforcement and security with the Diplomatic Security Service. During this time, he spent 11 years working in five countries and has visited more than 40. He specializes in emergency management and continuity of operations. He teaches as an adjunct faculty at George Mason University. He is happily married and has two teenage children.

Back in July 2020, we were four months into work-from-home. I had grown frustrated and, as often happens, my frustration manifested as anger: speaking sharply to those around me and kicking my inner critic into high gear. I was alienating myself from my friends and family. I knew I needed to make a change, so I took a long weekend when my wife and kids were traveling as a personal retreat. I reread a book that once inspired me, used a meditation app, and took some time to examine what was causing my frustration. I soon discovered that my singular focus on success from my work was detracting from succeeding in other areas of my life. I also realized that working from home offered a tremendous opportunity to broaden my perspective and focus on things that mattered to me as much as my career. I started exploring other areas of interest, broadened my network of contacts, and got involved in some new activities.

When I'm at work, I focus on work, to the exclusion of personal projects and priorities. It's part of my ethical core. But since I was working from home, a few things had changed: my agency declared that core hours no longer needed to be worked sequentially, and because I was no longer in the office using government equipment — my personal projects were much more accessible in the lulls between core hours.

During these lulls, I started exploring LinkedIn more, looking up friends and colleagues I had not been in touch with for a while. I came across a post from my friend Steve about an interview he did with Ron Worman, who hosts "The Great Conversation" podcast. (Check it out!) I let Steve know how great I thought the interview was, and he put me in touch with Ron. Ron and I had a conversation that he ended up recording for his subscribers. That connection with Ron had a domino effect. I continued to engage in the larger conversation taking place on his platform and write about what we discussed. After a while, Ron's encouragement helped me feel that I have a valuable voice of my own.

Previously, Ron interviewed Tim for the same podcast. Much of the content of their chat hit home for me, so I reached out to Tim on LinkedIn. A couple weeks later, Tim and Lee started The Kindness Games. Connecting with new leadership communities, my empowering conversation with Ron, and the work I did on my own to process my frustration and anger put me in a great place to appreciate The Kindness Games mission. I wanted in!

I watched as the community grew but hesitated to participate. I was unsure of myself: would I look foolish? Would I embarrass myself? Would I appear unprofessional to my colleagues? (We are very serious people in a very serious job.) Would I run afoul of the rules for government employees on public speaking?

By early December, I couldn't wait any longer — I had to participate. But who would I highlight? What would I say? Did I even have 30 people to mention? What if I overlooked someone important? Just like the links in the chain that led me to connect with the mission, I needed to take this one step at a time.

I started by grabbing a piece of paper and numbering it one through 30. As I added names to my list, I focused on highlighting a diverse group of people — from all walks of human life and from all the areas and phases of my own life and development. I wanted to thank everyone who had inspired me, mentored me, or helped me along my path — not just in my job, but as a person — to reflect my expanded priorities. As I grew through my frustration, I realized family and friends were as important to my success as mentors in my profession.

I recorded and posted my first three days. Watching them back, I realized I needed to bring more energy to the entries. So, on day four the first thing that came out of my mouth was, "THIS is The Kindness Games, and TODAY I want to highlight. . ." It was completely unplanned but with that, I was up and running. I had some minor variations, but quickly settled into my new intro for my videos.

A Broader Impact

Though I had a list, I didn't go in order. I was hesitant about some people due to their position. Some I think about often but hadn't actually spoken to in years. Each day, I would look at my list and ask, "Who today, Lord?" Sometimes the answer was immediate with a flash of inspiration of what to say. Other days, I would think about it all day and the answer wouldn't come until late in the evening. Sometimes it was surprising because the person wasn't even on my list! Others on my list are still waiting for the right inspired time. When I settled on the person, my next request was, "Lord, please give me the words." I knew I had to be careful with my content, but at the same time, the people I highlighted deserved it, so I couldn't hesitate indefinitely out of fear.

Several of the people I highlighted left kind comments on the post. Others called me directly to express their appreciation, some in tears because they had no idea that they had left the kind of impact that would lead to such a public appreciation. Many said it made their day, and several told me it had made their week. A handful told me that the timing of the post was perfect, as they had been struggling with work or personal issues, and this little shout-out was the ray of kindness cutting through to help them keep going. I was also surprised by the number of people who never clicked the "like" button or left a comment but would mention the posts to me in conversation; the impact is broader than it appears or than we realize.

These videos not only helped the people I highlighted. They also changed me. As I mentioned, I was hesitant to engage in The Kindness Games. In addition to being a "serious person in a serious profession," I work in what many people refer to as a "fear-based environment." You never want to say the wrong thing to someone who in the future might be in a position in which they can affect your future assignment or promotion. This leads to risk aversion. As part of processing my frustration, I decided to stop being afraid and to then model that decision. Engaging in this journey was part of that.

Even though I'm a government employee, I'm still a private citizen with my own voice. I've been working the past year to embrace that and use my voice for good through teaching, writing, and now, The Kindness Games. One of the things I've discovered is that I simply need to include the disclaimer, "The comments and opinions are my own and may not reflect those of my agency of the U.S. Government." (See how I managed to slip this disclaimer in, even here?)

I'm still working my way through TKG overtime, and instead of getting shorter, my list keeps getting longer. I keep connecting with people from my past or new people who inspire me. I probably add two people to my list for every new video I record. Being part of The Kindness Games Alumni community has been fantastic. It's such an interesting, fun, and supportive group of people. It's an honor to call them friends.

There's a quote attributed to Albert Schweitzer that I think perfectly captures the spirit of The Kindness Games,

"At times our own light goes out and is rekindled by a spark from another person. Each of us has cause to think with deep gratitude of those who have lighted the flame within us."

To which I exhort you: be the light; spread kindness.

Chapter 8: Kindness Begets Kindness Logarithmically

by Michael Gips, Principal, Global Insights in Professional Security

Michael Gips is a security executive, attorney, writer, researcher, trainer, and association professional. He was named the number one most influential thought leader in security by IFSEC Global in 2022 and one of the most influential people in security by Security Magazine in 2019. In 2021 he received the Outstanding Security Performance Award for U.S. Security Consultant.

It must have been the third or fourth challenge that made me tune out. The internet has spawned dozens of challenges, most of which I had succeeded in ignoring. A few years ago, my daughters eventually eroded my resistance until I agreed to go under the bucket of ice water for ALS, because it raised awareness for a good cause. A couple of months later, I eagerly knocked out 25 pushups for 25 days to shed light on PTSD.

But was I really aiding these causes or simply succumbing to trends? How meaningful was my participation?

As a fitness enthusiast, I didn't need a provocation to do pushups.

Other challenges poured forth, but all seemed to be self-serving spectacles, dangerous follies, or juvenile pranks. The 10-year photo challenge? Hard pass. Likewise to Birdbox, Mannequin, and their ilk.

So, when The Kindness Games hashtags, posts, and videos started appearing on my LinkedIn feed, they didn't make it through my credibility filter. As well-intentioned as the effort might have been, to me it was another trifling, time-sucking trend no one would remember in a month or two.

It Starts with Letting Kindness In

Yet The Kindness Games didn't fade, and the names of some of the participants seeped into the periphery of my consciousness. I knew Paul "Always Care" Moxness, and it made sense that he was taking part, because he may be the friendliest and most gracious person in security. And Myn Kyriannis, a cybersecurity expert, was taking part as well. Then I noticed Jonathon Harris, who had spoken on ESRM at a conference I held for ASIS's CSO Center. Interesting, but they were probably praising an inner circle of security pals in a mutual admiration society. Angela Scalpello, an executive coach I had gotten to know at a conference, also came aboard, which further piqued my interest. Still, I resisted.

It took Tim Wenzel's videos for the light to break through. Tim, who I knew from his work at Facebook and with ASIS was a natural showman, and the joy and energy of his shout-outs resonated. Here was someone unashamedly, enthusiastically saying nice things about people. A corporate guy, at that. Even when giving praise, we're used to acting "professionally," offering a nod of acknowledgement, a private word of support, and moving on. Tim was making theater out of it, and it was a revelation.

In fact, we live in a culture that has its priorities reversed: we praise in private and criticize in public. Blistering comments on blog posts and articles draw the most attention. Tolerance is out; divisiveness and warfare — class, intellectual, political, religious, and countless other types — are in.

The Kindness Games offers a reprieve and a reset.

Much of my work as a security consultant involves disinformation and misinformation, to the extent where I witness neighbors not even agreeing on objective truth. Animosity over everything such as face masks, guns, vaccines, civil justice protests, or gender was fraying the fabric of our society. For me, it was time to publicly sing the praises of good people, even if many of those people held polar views on critical topics. It was time to celebrate our commonality and goodness, not stoke another thing to divide us.

Getting Started

Now that I knew I would participate, how could I enter this inner circle? I hadn't been invited. I reached out to Tim, and he welcomed me unreservedly — no invitation needed. We would do a joint video to get me started, then I'd do the next 29 on my own. My goal was 30 posts in 30 consecutive days.

But I didn't want to be a tedious talking head people would scroll right by. I needed an angle to make sure my honorees would be noticed. By coincidence, I had recently written a column in *Security Magazine* arguing that a good leader should laud their staff in public, particularly by nominating them for professional awards.

That was it. I couldn't possibly nominate even a small fraction of deserving security professionals for official industry commendations, so I would highlight them in my videos and fashion my own "awards." They would be jury-rigged, kluged awards using assorted knickknacks, gewgaws, and lagniappes from around my office and house.

For example, my fourth video praised Ilya Umanskiy, known for his deep thinking on security issues. He was awarded a mini replica of Rodin's *The Thinker* sculpture that sits on a shelf in my office. A couple days later, I presented Marco Vega from Costa Rica with a snow globe reading "Pura Vida," the motto of that Central American land and Marco's personal catchphrase.

To keep some logic to the sequence, I arranged the honors in groups of three. For example, videos seven, eight, and nine recognized people from small countries in Northern Europe (Netherlands, Denmark, Belgium). Videos 10 through 12 congratulated security professionals who had just gotten new jobs, 20 through 22 covered healthcare security professionals, and so on.

For the first two weeks, my videos averaged between 600 and 1,000 views. Episode 15 changed my thinking about what could be done.

Making Things Interesting

Industry icon Chuck Andrews publicly challenged me to wear a full hockey uniform during my next video. (I play ice hockey in a local recreational league.) That included a helmet, shoulder pads, elbow pads, gloves, hockey pants, suspenders, and a jersey. Whether or not I wore skates shall forever remain a secret. The sheer bizarreness of the video attracted more than 2,500 views. Because this gimmick would draw attention away from the day's recipient, I picked someone who wouldn't mind — my older brother, Steve. For his forbearance, he got a plastic Mark Messier of the Rangers holding the 1994 Stanley Cup.

Inspired by the reaction to this offbeat approach, I filmed three episodes while I was in New Orleans moving my daughter into her off-campus college housing. I took a video after running in Audubon Park to honor jogging enthusiast Ricky Gordon and appeared on the grounds of Tulane University to call out Tulane adjunct instructor James DeMeo.

In the meantime, devotees of The Kindness Games were liking and commenting on the posts, encouraging me on the journey. Lee Oughton led the way. A comment on my hockey video by Kathleen Fariss, whom I had never met, reflected and redoubled kindness back at me. She wrote: "What courage and intentionality this took to not only tape, but to post. Your leadership with this is going to spark a whole new wave and I am sure you were not thinking that when you posted this! Go you! Keep rocking it and showing up for you, us, and the world!!" Who wouldn't be energized by that kind of love? Kathleen showed me that kindness begets kindness logarithmically.

Kathleen continued to inspire me, as did Paul Moxness, Al Robinette, Kelsey Carnell, Lee Oughton, and others. In fact, I used my 30th episode to call out 18 people who had regularly commented on the posts, resulting in a whirlwind episode in which I had to find prizes for 18 people — among them a bag of Skittles, a ghost emoji, and a lacrosse ball.

COVID-19 cruelly intruded and hijacked the levity, however. Dr. Ona Ekhonu, a security pioneer in Nigeria and West Africa at large, succumbed to the disease during my 30 days of videos. He received his own somber yet celebratory tribute, one of many that deservedly surfaced on social media.

Reactions from the honorees I recognized were fascinating. Most wrote kind and gracious comments in response. Some continued to follow my journey, liking or commenting on subsequent posts. Some honorees liked the post without commenting. A few never responded at all — they probably hadn't been on LinkedIn, or perhaps they didn't like the attention or wished to remain humble.

When I posted in honor of R.C. Miles, the head of security for the AIDS Healthcare Foundation, I resorted to an easy pun: I started by reciting Robert Frost's poem that ends, "And miles to go before I sleep."

My first 30 posts barely touched on the people in my life worthy of a shout of public recognition. I indeed have miles to go before I exhaust my contribution to The Kindness Games. And it sure beats a bucket of ice water over the head.

Chapter 9: A Community United in Kindness

by Sue Ginsburg, Austin, TX

Sue Ginsburg is the Client Success Specialist for Intrycks Website and Digital Marketing and has more than 30 years of experience in Strategic Growth Marketing. She works collaboratively, leveraging people's individual strengths. A big believer in creating "win-win" situations, Sue always seeks the positive and strives to insert kindness into everyday life, including doing Random Acts of Kindness.

It was six months into the COVID-19 pandemic, and as summer weather cooled down, I could feel my positivity waning. I hadn't seen my kids or family for a year; I had only seen a handful of friends, and I missed human contact. George Floyd's death was bringing out negativity and riots too close to home — literally, for me, living in Minneapolis at the time. The pandemic was getting to me.

When my friend Steve mentioned this thing called The Kindness Games, my ears perked up. Something new, something positive, something I could do. I was in.

Setting a Focus for the Day

When I started creating a list of people who stood out for their kindness, I didn't have to look far. My sister-in-law and brother, for example, had shown extra TLC since the pandemic hit, because they knew I lived by myself. My daughter and I, each living by ourselves, had created some rituals to be together via video during the day, which helped break up our time spent alone. When I was feeling isolated, their extra kindness meant the world to me. This was a good start, and it left me space to add as I got into the 30 days of The Kindness Games.

An amateur at recording myself, it took me five to seven takes each time for my first few posts before I would have something that felt acceptable. I got better with time, but I also quickly realized that it was the message, not the method, that people cared about.

Posting a video became part of my morning routine. Quite unexpectedly, I found it set the stage for focusing on kindness throughout my day. Talking about kindness every morning was uplifting and set a positive tone for the day. This is always good, but during the pandemic, it was like a boost of adrenaline even before my morning coffee.

Finding Community

Participating in The Kindness Games gave me a feeling of belonging to something. When the pandemic had taken away live gatherings, this community was a haven. Reading their posts and the ensuing comments each day got me into conversations with people I didn't know, yet we already had a strong bond in common — sharing kindness. I felt I belonged to something bigger than me, to a worldwide movement. The Kindness Games participants, people I might never have crossed paths with, became people I knew and respected. It was magic.

Posting each day also helped me reconnect with friends and colleagues from near and far. Kindness is a novelty to see on a professional platform like LinkedIn, so people noticed it. Interestingly, my most-viewed posts were the two most personal ones I shared — one about my three kids and our pandemic practice of weekly video calls, and one about my "step dog," a pandemic puppy who taught me the remarkable benefits of loving a dog.

All in all, I experienced firsthand the ripple effect that sharing simple acts of kindness can have. I saw kindness unite people from all over the world. I saw kindness create a community in The Kindness Games. I saw kindness bring people I knew and didn't know smiles and laughter. It brought light at a dark time. Never underestimate the power a smile or kind word may have, pandemic or not. As Dr. Seuss said,

"To the world, you may be one person;
but to one person, you may be the world."

KEY TAKEAWAYS

Wait, What the Fun?

1	**Be the light.** Uplift and inspire others by being the light in their day/week/year. You'll find that it uplifts and inspires you, too.
2	**Embrace creativity.** Be your own unique self. Find ways to be creative when you're feeling stuck or uninspired.
3	**Establish kindness as part of your routine.** Set aside time to be intentional with kindness. You can do this at any time and throughout your day, but the beginning or end of your day are good places to start.

The Good, Bad, and Ugly: Feedback

Zero sum: a situation, often cited in game theory, in which one person's gain is equivalent to another's loss. This seems to be a popular world view. If someone wins or does well, it must be at the expense of another's loss. The haves and the have nots perspective is based on domination over others. As a result, those who are not "doing well" in life feel helpless. Taken to the extreme, it paints a grim picture of our fellow humans and their motives. This perspective can rear its ugly head when people feel ill-treated.

In this world, there is no evidence that we are in a zero-sum game. While some people lead their lives this way, it is not the rule. If a billionaire's net worth increases by another billion dollars, it didn't get yanked out of someone else's savings. If I lose my job, it's not because someone else took it from me. When the haters come out against us — among other contributors, as you've already read in the previous sections — because we stand for leading with kindness, it doesn't change us. Even though haters mean to keep us down, embarrass us, and suppress our voices. . . it doesn't matter. Why?

There is a universal truth in life — If you want to identify your greatest obstacle, look in the mirror. You must choose how you react to life and how you allow life to affect you.

The X

The X is the perfect place for an ambush. It's the most ideal place for your enemies to trap you, where they hold the advantage and your fate is left to chance. The X is the most dangerous place in the universe for you.

Tim and Lee have trained to identify and avoid the X their entire lives. As soldiers, high-threat security contractors, and executive protection professionals, they have lived with the reality that people are watching them, plotting their destruction, and marking their X. As a necessity, they've trained and have taught others how to react to an ambush. Their mantra is to get off the X and move. By making just two to three moves (physically from a security standpoint, conversationally from a professional standpoint), you have a much greater chance of getting out of the situation.

Your X could be reacting to an unfair comment. It could be a mandatory meeting. It might be a person who commonly disagrees with you or makes assumptions about you.

When someone has chosen to dominate your narrative, they've chosen and designed your X for a sure victory. After the opening hit, they're confident. They gauge your reaction and disposition, so they can coordinate their next move. Stand up in front of them and choose not to follow their script. Choose not to cower and fade away, not to conform to a restrictive community, and instead, calmly choose to move.

History of the X

How can you survive the perfect lethal setup? It all comes down to three moves that you make. The initiation of an ambush is designed for two things:

1. **To kill and injure as many people as possible in the opening attack**

2. **For the violence to be so intense that it disorients and paralyzes the survivors, so they are easy prey for the second phase**

In those opening moments, when you're the target of an ambush, your survival is left to fate — you have about a 50-50 chance of survival. There is little you can do outside of the preparation and strategy you've already implemented.

As the first phase deadens, if you've survived, there's an opportunity to make a choice. Where should I go? "Get off the X!" is our mantra during training. Is your vehicle still operational? Drive off the X. Do you need to get out of your vehicle? Where should you immediately run to? Once there, choose the next place and run. Then once more.

If you can execute two to three decisions to move, your chances of survival border 90 percent. Survivors have even run into the ambushing force and survived. Sometimes one or two people accidentally become a counter-ambush to the enemy force, breaking it up and saving their friends. In fact, a strong tactic for surviving an ambush — if you know where it originated — is assault straight into the enemy force to overwhelm them.

Before your week begins, look at your calendar. As you organize your agenda for the week, contemplate where your Xs are. We focus on two types of activities: the ones you're excited to do and the ones you dread.

The activities you're excited about carry pitfalls because we don't consider who else is involved and what they're hoping to experience. Sometimes we show up so excited that we take all the energy for ourselves, unknowingly pushing others to the periphery and unintentionally stealing their experience.

Conversely, the activities or scenarios we dread are more obvious. Something about them induces fear, anxiety, or complete boredom. We don't prepare for them and instead hope they go as well as they can. Hope won't get you off the X. Only the strategic preparations you have made before walking into the ambush will serve as a buffer.

On Sunday, survey your week and identify potential Xs. Let's prepare our strategy:

1. What is my purpose for this scenario? What do I want to accomplish? What are my best outcomes? What are acceptable outcomes?
2. Who will be participating in these scenarios with me? List them.

Now from their perspective:

1. What do I think their purpose is? What do they wish to accomplish? What are their best outcomes? What are their acceptable outcomes?
2. What are the best common scenarios among all of us?
3. What's my role? What's within my ability to help design these outcomes for us?

When we try to align our purpose with the purposes of others, we can begin to understand what tensions may arise, what problems may be on the horizon, and what ideas may work to avoid or lessen these issues in the moment. As the scenario progresses, if we engage our curiosity and ask these types of questions, we can lead a common vision to a common goal. We allow everyone to participate and provide their input and perspective. By doing this, we change the dynamics of these scenarios and lessen the chances of attack or misunderstanding.

We can't let others' negative perceptions and criticisms darken our vision. It can be painful to hear unkind words and sentiments, but it often tells us that the person has more going on beneath the surface. Be leaning into our vulnerability, staying curious, and giving others the benefit of the doubt, we can accept that we don't understand why the person negatively affecting us is doing so. Seek to understand what's contributing to their negative energy, and be there if and when they decide to let you in. In the meantime, focus on the support you do have, keep growing your community with the people who are eager to join it, and keep spreading kindness to all.

In This Section

Notice how the positive feedback is so invigorating for Brandon and Kunle and how it gives them renewed energy. Margo's encounter with negative feedback is not so uncommon for our alumni — as you've read in previous sections — and in fact admits to being a hater at first as well! (Those haters-turned-engagers are our favorites by the way.) Margo reminds us, "What I learned from this is that people who aren't happy with themselves will be unhappy with you when you start to work on yourself." Sometimes those who judge you aren't ready to do what you're doing, and that makes them uncomfortable and scared. Spread more kindness their way, not less.

Chapter 10: Kindness as Self-Care

by Margo Cash, Talent Acquisition Professional

Margo Cash is in talent acquisition at Houzz, a global start-up, where she creates inclusive and accessible hiring processes that prioritize diversity, empathy, and transparency. She lives in Los Angeles with her husband and her rescue dog, Oatmeal, where you'll find her planning her next international adventure. Margo earned degrees in Art Business and Art History.

In June 2021, I was in a completely different place than I am now. I was sitting in my new-ish apartment office, staring out the window, and wondering what in the world I was doing with my life. Every single person has gone through challenges since COVID-19 started, and while I had not faced job loss, financial issues, or the death of loved ones, I wasn't in a good place mentally.

In August 2020, I had received two job offers, and I chose the job I knew I could do instead of the one that would be a leap for me. I guess I shouldn't have been surprised when, a few months later, I found myself facing some of the same issues I'd already been facing, in the same industry as before, and feeling awful about myself. My turning point was when I was driving one afternoon and thought to myself, *Well, I could just drive off the side of the road, and it would all be over.* This was around the holidays, and that passing thought scared me more than anything in the world.

I had hit a low in self-esteem, self-care, and self-respect. I didn't believe in what I was doing, I was getting relentlessly bullied at work, and I was damaging relationships with my friends and family because I was overworked and depressed. I drove home, told my husband what had gone through my head, and found a therapist.

Keep Doing the Work

I wish I could say that was the end of the low points, but nothing changes without hard work. I started therapy, and it became evident that I had to quit the job that was contributing to harming my psychological safety. I returned to the organization I had left for that job licking my wounds and feeling like a failure. I kept quiet. I avoided telling my mentor what was going on because I was afraid he would be disappointed in me. I was just thankful to have a place to land financially, and I got back to the work I knew how to do.

Of course, there were some highlights to the pandemic — adopting my 8-year-old shelter dog Oatmeal, spending more time with my husband, and being able to cook more — but other obstacles came into my path. I was severely fatigued and facing some health challenges that required lots of tests — including a heart monitor I had to wear for quite some time, wrecking my skin. I also started to face challenges at work again. It felt like a broken record with no room for innovation or growth, and my voice was being stifled again. I was miserable, and I started to think, *Is it me?* Well, partially it was!

I started to hop on LinkedIn more and noticed Kathleen Farris doing some pretty cool videos. She was shouting-out people in her network, but I didn't fully understand why. I knew she had started her own business, and I was just proud of her for getting out there and being visible in front of the internet. But then Suzanne, one of my colleagues at work, made a post.

I was working late on something and got a notification that I had been tagged. I watched Suzanne's post a few times, tears welling up in my eyes. Someone thought I was that special? Someone took the time to say these nice things about me and actually post this on LinkedIn? What was The Kindness Games? I texted her to say thank you, and we planned to check in the next day so she could tell me all about TKG.

Suzanne's post had bolstered my spirits, but even something so good couldn't seem to stick with me forever. By the time we met, I was feeling skeptical again. She explained what The Kindness Games was and how Kathleen had introduced her to it. I found myself at another small crossroads: simply thank Suzanne for her post and go about my week? Or jump in and do it, too? I chose the latter.

I wish I could say I was thinking about long-term outcomes when I said "yes," but in reality, I am just used to saying "yes" to things. I thought it could be fun. The message of TKG resonated with me, and it seemed easy enough. But I know in the back of my mind, I was itching for something new — a safe space to do something different and a way to make a change. After all, I was once again miserable except for the nice compliments Suzanne had given me. What did I have to lose?

The Journey Is Better than the Destination

I started my own Kindness Games journey a few days later, not wanting to lose the momentum from my conversation with Suzanne. I started to check out how TKG had originated and watched others' posts to get some inspiration. Because I had been missing travel so much, I decided to use Zoom to record my posts, so the backgrounds in my videos could be somewhere I had traveled, if only to spark some joyous memories.

I was a nervous wreck as I booted up Zoom and filmed my first post about my colleague and friend, Jill. I had to start and stop a few times, but I tried to make the video as authentic as possible. I watched it back and stared at myself on the screen. *Do I really look and sound like that?* I thought. *This is stupid! Why am I putting myself out there?* I had a full-blown negative self-talk rant and then uploaded the video anyway, tagging Jill and praying that she wouldn't think it was weird.

To my surprise, she thought it was cool and was grateful for it. And people liked my post. And I didn't die. Nothing bad happened whatsoever. And it made me feel nice for a few minutes to talk about someone I care about.

Okay, I told myself. Let's keep doing this.

I carefully thought through my connections and relationships. I was deliberate in my selections and narrowed it down to a list of 29 other people to talk about. I chose some folks I love and respect to the core and feel an inherent need to tell the world about; some folks I hadn't connected with in a while, and I wanted to make sure they knew how much of an impact they had left on me; and some folks I didn't necessarily have the best relationships with, but wasn't too proud to share how awesome they are at their work. This last group of people was important to me — I have always struggled with FOMO (fear of missing out) and jealousy, feeling like I am not up to speed with my peers. I intentionally forced myself to go out of my comfort zone and recognize truly awesome people I felt intimidated by.

After I started making videos, my reason for doing The Kindness Games shifted dramatically. No longer was it about fulfilling a promise to Suzanne, but it became almost an essential part of my self-care routine. It felt like therapy. It felt freeing. It felt like it was going to change my life.

And it did.

The Gifts of TKG

Maybe it sounds silly, but I didn't expect to be so holistically transformed by my experience with The Kindness Games. I know that the whole idea of TKG was to spread more kindness in the world at a time when things were so bleak and divided. But for me, The Kindness Games changed my life. I'd been a skeptic who didn't exactly feel like making happy and positive posts on LinkedIn. I didn't really feel like complimenting people. Why? Because I didn't even like myself. I was nervous, scared, self-conscious, and knew that I was partially to blame for why I was feeling so stuck in my career and my life. No matter how many personality or career change tests I took, nothing seemed to solve my problems or make me any happier in my day-to-day life. When Suzanne made her post about me, I really broke down. I had love from friends, family, and my husband, but this felt different. For someone to really see me at work and in my professional life felt different.

As I participated in The Kindness Games, every shout-out I made brought me something. I don't say this to mean that I wanted things from the challenge, but the gifts of doing it fell into my lap anyway. I was able to get vulnerable, like in the post I made about a mentor I was afraid I had disappointed. He reached out, and we got our professional relationship back on track. I was able to shout-out colleagues and see how it brightened their week in real time at work. I was able to reconnect with past colleagues, friends, and peers and hear about their lives and journeys since we'd last spoken. And with the folks I was intimidated by, I gained a sense of peace, and the one-sided competition I had felt melted away.

I was also able to expand my network. Shortly after I started, Suzanne and I hosted a professional development Zoom meeting with our female-identifying colleagues at work and invited Kehkashan, Kelsey, and Kathleen to the conversation. Since another one of my colleagues named Heidi had decided to join The Kindness Games as well, we all did a joint shout-out together. It was so fun to be in community together and allow ourselves to be vulnerable. The network just kept on giving. Being able to cheer for others and have them cheer for me was a great feeling.

Every day my connections grew and deepened. Every day my eyes and heart opened, and my confidence bloomed. I finished my 30 posts with a special video for my husband, who had cheered me on along my journey behind the scenes. I know this journey isn't over for me.

Haters Gonna Hate

I was able to do a joint shout-out with Tim Wenzel, one of the founders, and get to know his story before sharing it. While we talked, he asked me if I had gotten any negative feedback while posting. I didn't exactly know what he meant at that time. I was 17 posts in, everyone was loving it, and I was feeling great! Hate? What hate?

But sometimes, "hate" isn't a nasty comment on your LinkedIn post. It can be subtler than that, and I soon started to become aware of changes in those around me. My true champions were there pushing me forward, proud of me, and loving that I was transforming into a better version of myself by letting kindness lead me. People saw that I wasn't as quiet anymore. I wasn't the Margo many had gotten to know or expect. I was becoming Margo 2.0, open and learning and healing and sharing — but that didn't sit well with some people.

The louder my voice got — in other words, the more confidence I had to speak up in meetings at work, innovate, go my own way, and have a solid presence on LinkedIn — the more I was criticized and told I wasn't meeting expectations in my job. This connection became clear right around when I hit my 30 posts. Some people were not on board with what I was doing.

What I learned from this is that people who aren't happy with themselves will be unhappy with you when you start to work on yourself. I know this because I was one of those people in June 2021, before I started making changes in my life. But by August, I could clearly see and recognize in others the same negative patterns of behavior I used to have. Am I perfect? No. But I learned that when people are talking behind your back, putting you down, or trying to silence you, it is a "them" problem, not a "you" problem.

One of the reasons I was so upset and dissatisfied before my TKG journey was because people were not being kind to me. But I needed to take responsibility. It's not anyone's duty to be kind to me. (Although we should all spread kindness!) TKG was the perfect way to change my perspective. I could give kindness to others without expecting anything in return. I could make them feel the way I wanted to feel or tell them what I wished someone would tell me. I could make an impact and help others make an impact. As cliché as it sounds, I could be the change I wished to see in the world.

Kindness is a superpower. You can be kind and introverted or extroverted or anything in between. You can be kind and just starting your career, or kind and a CEO. Kindness is a choice, not a weakness.

The Kindness Games changed my life, and I'm excited to share it with the world. I know now that the most important things are working on the needs of my soul and sharing respect and kindness with the world, and especially with those who need it.

The Journey Continues

If you would've told me two months ago that I would be sitting here with peace in my heart, a new job offer in hand, new friends, and vast opportunity, I would have laughed. And not just a giggle, but a hearty, side-splitting laugh. But that's now my reality.

The Kindness Games was a small chance I took on myself. I almost think of it as a micro-step. I started posting videos and spending only 15 minutes a day on the whole process, but everything else started to snowball in a positive way. I felt better in my soul, so I also wanted to feel better in general, so I picked up exercising again. I felt lighter and less depressed, so I got back into my hobbies. I felt more loving and open, so my relationship with my husband got deeper. I realized that words matter, and time is of the essence, so I shared how I felt with friends and family. I started to see my worth and that kindness was a strength and not a weakness, and I exercised the kindness muscle at work.

I also got my passion and joy back and knew in my heart that change was my responsibility. I started going out of my comfort zone and asking new connections on LinkedIn to meet for a virtual coffee and chat. One of these meetings turned into an interview, which turned into a job offer in a field I have been trying to break into for a while — all because someone saw one of my videos and recognized my inherent gifts of connection and empathy. Someone saw my value, honored my journey, and gave me an opportunity. I'm excited for this new role and chance to shine and grow. I'm also excited to keep building relationships within the TKG community, share the message of TKG, and head into overtime. I can pursue all of these things because of this amazing movement and how I opened myself to it and allowed it to change me for the better.

Know that those who are unkind or do not support you walking in kindness are fighting their own battles. Keep giving them kindness no matter what. But remember that kindness is free, and it's just as important to give it to others as it is to give it to yourself.

Trust in the process, be vulnerable, and enjoy the ride!

Chapter 11: Recognize Your Impact

by Brandon Tan, The Kindness Games Alumnus

Brandon Tan is a tech industry professional with program management expertise. He builds and scales projects, engages stakeholders, and prioritizes kindness in his leadership approach. Brandon participates in The Kindness Games to inspire positive change. He also has a passion for fashion and completed Fashion Business courses at Parsons School of Design. He is always open to connecting.

An Unexpected Message

9/16/20 9:31 AM from Tim Wenzel, co-creator of The Kindness Games and colleague at Facebook:

> Hey man, how have you been? I was thinking about you the other day. I recently kicked off #TheKindnessGames and it seems right up your alley, random posts of kindness to counteract our world of insanity. . . Check it out! I thought you might be interested. You're the happiest dude I know.

My response:

> Thanks again Tim! Like what you're doing now with the #TheKindnessGames; you're creating something that spreads a positive culture. If I have the chance to spread a positive germ around, why not?

To be honest, I wasn't expecting this message at all. I have never really worked directly with Tim nor (I thought) did I even have a working relationship with him. I had worked with his team but not Tim directly. Back when I was in a reception position at Facebook, I worked in the corporate security building and made sure to memorize every single person who worked in that building. It pleasantly surprised most people who passed my desk. I always tried to be the light in the room, and eventually it paid off — I ended up being promoted into another role as an Event Coordinator. Everything I had been doing had a positive impact. This taught me that my conduct and behavior have had impact, no matter how minor I thought they were. I was just trying to do my job well, not expecting any outcome other than making the individuals in my building feel special. For those reading this, wherever you may be in your life, you have influence — even if you don't believe it.

Tim reaching out to me about The Kindness Games was one of the best things to have happened to me in my professional life. It has boosted my courage, self-image, and public speaking skills. The thing is, when Tim reached out to me about The Kindness Games, I didn't want to do it. At all. I didn't have the courage at the time. It wasn't until Tim posted his Day 14 TKG episode when that all changed. . .

9/17/20 8:34 AM Tim posts:

> Day 14 — Brandon Tan

I was flabbergasted. I never realized how much of an impact I had on Tim and others. After watching Tim's Day 14 TKG post, I knew I had to start the challenge as well. To be honest, doing anything outside of work was not my forte. So, participating in a challenge that I would have to do in my spare time wasn't preferable. However, I had to acknowledge the obligation I felt to spread more positivity, especially during COVID-19 lockdowns. Positive impact outweighed my own fear. It was time to record and post.

I spent time learning about iMovie, editing, and visual techniques. I spent even more time thinking about who I was going to highlight first and what I would say about them. At first, I was concerned about what I was going to say about others, but I just thought about who had impacted me in my life whether that be professionally or personally. After some courage, video editing, and extra hours. . . Bam. I posted my Day 1 of The Kindness Games on LinkedIn. I pretty much copied the format of Tim's and Lee's episode structure, but with added visuals. This elevated the challenge, as Lee started using amazing video edits to level the playing field. I spoke from the heart, but still had to write a structure and script, as I was not perfect at recording without one. But, progress and completion happened nonetheless.

I couldn't believe the response to my first video. It got so many reactions and responses to it. Positive impact really worked, even virtually. I started getting tons of connection invitations on LinkedIn, and my network started growing.

About Me

I'm 25 years old and come from a very non-traditional professional background. I attended a medical high school and intended to attend college and eventually join the pharmaceutical field. However, due to financial hardship at the time, I could no longer support that dream. My father found that people my age (then 19 to 21) were making the same in a career (if not more than) as employees with recent college degrees, so he wanted me to skip the expense and get right into the workforce. This was probably the best thing that could've happened to me in those difficult circumstances, although I didn't see it that way at the time.

After graduating high school, I spent six months working at this horrible sushi restaurant. The restaurant was always understaffed, and our paychecks would even bounce sometimes. I don't know why no one ever took legal action against the owners, but that's just how it was.

Fortunately, my older brother mentioned roles available at contract companies working for other major companies. One of them contracted with Facebook. I applied for the role and got it! For about two years I commuted 140 miles to work every day, leaving at 3 am and getting home at 7, 8, or 9 pm depending on traffic. I was setting the foundation for my family's future stability and working hard for it.

Five years later, I'm a full-time employee at Meta (previously Facebook) and have been able to support myself and my family, which is an absolute blessing. I have learned so much working at a major tech company and am still learning every day. I have been able to move a lot closer to work and am grateful for the opportunities I have been given to prove myself despite my lack of traditional on-paper experience and education.

With all this being said, I did everything for my family and honestly did not think about others as much. When The

Kindness Games showed up, I knew it was a chance to make up for it and spread the love virtually!

The Journey

The Kindness Games challenge wasn't easy. It taught me to be accountable for things I promise to do even when I'm not required to do them. This challenge was completely optional, but I knew I had a self-imposed obligation to complete it. My consistency was not perfect, but it did get done. Though the challenge is to post every day for 30 days, I didn't do that at all. I typically would post every other day or during the weekend. It took me about two months to complete the entire challenge, but the message was still received. I got messages from all those I shouted-out, and it was great to reconnect with everyone. There were some I shouted-out who I hadn't spoken to or seen in what felt like forever.

On top of impacting those I shouted out, I also had a time to connect with so many new people such as Joshua Ladesma, Lee Oughton, and Kelsey Carnell. I got to learn more about the corporate security industry outside of private tech and so much more. The Kindness Games challenge had inspired me to take on more than I thought I could handle. I've improved my skills in video editing, public speaking, and leadership. Because of the confidence this challenge gave me, I'm currently on the board at my company's Toastmasters chapter, and I've attained new certifications to further my career in the corporate world. All this came about because of one unexpected message.

Chapter 12: Kindness Is Contagious

by Kunle Pelemo, Mental Health Strategist

Kunle Pelemo, also known as K.P., is a multi-talented and nation-building knowledge business strategist. He has been a down-to-earth and unconventional public speaker since 2002. He's the Lead Strategist of Mycarebuddy, an online mental health platform in Nigeria, and co-founder of Harmony Circle, an Indo-Nigerian collaboration for suicide prevention in Nigeria and India. Kunle champions his mental health and suicide prevention cause called Live And Not Die (LAND).

Sometime in November 2020 I got tagged by my friend Steve Donofrio on one of his Kindness Games posts on LinkedIn, calling me to get on board. I went through the post and found out it was all about one of the things I value so much in life: kindness. I immediately went through a couple of posts by Tim Wenzel and Lee Oughton, co-founders of The Kindness Games, to get further insight into the challenge. I started to think about how I could share my appreciation for a couple people who have been a blessing to me in one way or another, as well as recognize people I may not have met but for whose humanitarian works I have so much love.

No Reason Not to Join

As someone who's in humanitarian services, I know how an act of kindness is pivotal to changing a lot in our world today. The pandemic had shut down a lot of things across the world in the year The Kindness Games was founded. It further showed how much we all need one another to survive, as well as the need to grow a culture of kindness.

I'm a mental health advocate, so I also know how kindness helps both the giver and the receiver. There's an intimate connection between acts of kindness and one's mental health. This is something that makes TKG resonate well with me. The games offer a means of appreciating and connecting with people, something I already love to do. Why wouldn't I join?

Participating in TKG had multiple benefits: doing what I love, making others happy, and building a network of resourceful people across the world. I met so many wonderful people I wouldn't have met without TKG.

Being Kind to Others and Oneself

I create sensitization programs online. They're programs that work to make people more sensitive to and aware of certain issues, to improve knowledge, and build social support. So, I have a lot of people who have blessed me with their presence and resourcefulness on so many occasions. I was excited to have an international platform in The Kindness Games to show my appreciation and tag them in my posts. The only problem was how to narrow down my endless list to fit into 30 days.

I decided to maximize my time by tagging and shouting-out multiple people each day. I got the pictures of as many people as I could to recognize each day, put them together to upload, and talked about how each of them impacted me.

Tagging and appreciating brothers, friends, and other people whose work I admire online on my major social media platforms (LinkedIn, Facebook, and Instagram) was a great journey. I made each of the 30 posts at my own pace. After all, it's all about kindness, so being kind to oneself is part of the game. Yes, I missed a couple of days without posting, but I didn't have to beat myself up; I had to remain focused. With the help of Tim (who got on a video call with me), coupled with a shout-out from Lee, Kehkashan, and Kelsey, and engagements with my posts by other TKG members, I reached my goal. And then I kept going!

I did a few overtime posts, as we call it. My first OT post was a video I shot with Steve Donofrio during Christmas 2020. Steve wore a Santa outfit while I had the Santa hat on. It was fun. I also did an OT New Year's shout-out with my friend Phiwe in South Africa, which we used to wish Africa a Happy 2021.

Afterward, I had another remarkable OT with the ever-smiling Coach Kathleen Fariss, where we discussed mental health and leadership — a topic near and dear to our hearts. It gets no better than that.

Feedback

It's been established that the brain needs feedback in whatever we do; it keeps track of progress and helps our bodies secrete corresponding hormones in line with the feedback it's given. As the saying goes, progress equals happiness, so it was important to get feedback from the TKG posts in order to know their level of impact.

Well, kindness never disappoints. I got positive feedback on every single post I made. The feedback from the wonderful people I mentioned in my posts was absolutely amazing. They all loved it. Even better, other people who saw the posts used them as an opportunity to share their own appreciation for those I'd mentioned. It made everybody involved feel good. That speaks volumes about the contagiousness of kindness.

Effects of TKG

The Kindness Games was the best thing that happened to me in 2020. In a year where our world was badly hit by the pandemic, I also faced so many personal challenges. I lost my mum despite several efforts to rescue her earlier in that year. The Kindness Games came at just the right time for me. Suddenly, I saw a different perspective about showing kindness. Just the simple act of showing others you appreciate them goes a long way.

I'm hoping to start a service of kindness in my immediate environment where I can offer certain help services at a local store, organization, or community, free of charge.

We're creating a kindness explosion across the world. The more we show and receive kindness, the better our world would be. I'm ending this with the lyrics of a song, "Ride This Train" by The Canton Spirituals, that we used for voice training while I was in a singing group way back in school:

"Come along my friend,
come along get on board,
and ride this train.
Nothing on this train to lose,
everything to gain."

KEY TAKEAWAYS

The Good, Bad, and Ugly: Feedback

1 — **Deal with the haters.**
Haters will try to use false choices and pressure to keep you in a position or in a conversation. Learning to recognize their patterns will help you be prepared to engage and expertly redirect them in the moment of conflict.

2 — **Most people don't want to be bad people, bad employees, or bad bosses.**
There's usually pain somewhere that's causing their behavior. It doesn't excuse their behavior or actions, but it reminds us of their humanity and that we should send kindness their way.

3 — **Kindness is a superpower.**
Being kind gives you the power to take charge of your mindset, which impacts your day, and over time, will impact your life.

Change Your Mindset, Change Your World

A Word from Lee

 I had just finished a traditional English dinner of fish fingers, chips, and beans. Eager to get back to my playmates, I grabbed my coat and dashed out of the front door with ketchup still smeared across my face. I flung the gate open haphazardly, off to kick a ball around with my friends. In an instant I was in the middle of the road and SMASH —

 I was flying, hitting a car windscreen with such force that its front window cracked. In the blink of an eye, I was back in my front room completely dazed, like a cartoon character hit hard in the head with birds flying around them in circles. My mum was screaming at my dad, telling him I had blood streaming from my mouth. To my mother's relief, it was the ketchup from my fish fingers dinner.

 In the full story as told by the driver, I ran out into the street without looking. Before the driver could react, he hit me. I hit the windshield, slid down the front of the vehicle, got straight back up as if nothing had happened, and ran back into our house. The driver was clearly traumatized by what had just happened and came to the house, apologizing profusely for hitting me. (Though, clearly it was me who was in the wrong for not looking before running into the street.) My parents sympathized with him and consoled him. They reassured him that it was not his fault, and he couldn't have prevented the accident under the circumstances.

The next day, the driver returned to our home with a treasure trove of confectionary delights for yours truly. I thought Christmas had come early!

This event helped me understand the importance of kindness at an early age. As an adult, I look back on the accident with gratitude. The driver acted with such care and tenderness, and my parents showed empathy and forgiveness. I recall this incident as one of the most important teachable moments in my life: I learned that approaching every situation with kindness — even the terrible ones, and the ones that affect you personally — is key.

It even might've been the spark that eventually inspired The Kindness Games.

A Word from Tim

"Life is a series of ups and downs. We all get the same shot at it. Some people will enjoy life no matter what is going on. Other people will never have a day of fun in their entire life; because they choose it." – Duane Wenzel 1949-2018

My father raised me to understand that nothing is completely outside of our control. There are always things that we can do to move ourselves and others toward a better path. He told an angry kid that I got to choose how I felt and how I interacted with life and others, and that the outcomes I achieved were mine alone, and there would be no one but me to answer for these results.

These are bold words coming from the hardest working man I ever knew, who probably never brought home more than $50,000 a year for a family of four boys. He literally died working and never had a hope for retirement. He wanted the material things that most of us want, too, but never achieved them, because he made decisions which ensured he would never reach the financial independence that he craved. Yet there would be no one to blame other than the man in the mirror when bills were overdue, and when tough decisions needed to be made so we could survive. Not only did he own up to his results, he told me and my siblings exactly why we were struggling, but we were in it together.

If I could leave you with just one thought, one thing to hold onto, it would be this: You are responsible for the world around you, for your sphere of influence. There are people who look to you, people who want to be like you, and people you are responsible for in some way, even if not directly. A life well-lived is not for us, it's for the watchers. The people who quietly observe how you interact with your world. How you treat a waitress, talk about your boss, and speak to your spouse influences the people who emulate you when you don't realize it. A life well-lived sets an example of how to live well. Though it may be more difficult for you, you do it because it is right.

You might say, "No, I don't want this responsibility." The reality is you have it. No one asked you to model life for them, to model right and wrong for them. No one asked you to show them how to care for others or leave the world better than you found it. But you're being watched anyway, and your actions and inaction are instructive to others.

Duane Wenzel realized this. While he modeled many good things, he also modeled bad, but he owned his shortcomings. He spoke the truth about his failings and that there were better ways than he had found. There were better ways that he knew, yet for some reason couldn't do. We all aspire to things we will not attain. That does not make us failures, just human.

When we realize that our common humanity binds us tighter together than the forces which would divide us, we're stronger because of our shortcomings. Our flaws and reliance upon one another for strength and support highlight the beauty within our brokenness. When we realize there's only one human race, and that we are in this struggle called life together. . . What is your part? What is your purpose? Will you lead with kindness? Will you intentionally recognize the human on the other side of each life situation you engage in? It's impossible to escape life unscathed, unscarred, unbroken. But it is possible to attempt to tailor each life experience, as much as depends on you, to be the best possible experience for the humans on the other side.

What will you tell your children or your nieces and nephews, or the kid down the street who magically shows up each time you're in front of your home, and you have no idea why? What will you tell them when they ask you about the world around you, the one you're both experiencing? What will your part be?

In This Section

In these final stories, see how far kindness can go and what kind of world our TKG Alumni are contributing toward. Paul, Wanda, Elisa, and Kathleen share some incredible insights, ideas, and innovations. Consider how you'll embrace kindness and show up in your community — and the world.

Chapter 13: Beyond the Noise, Kindness is Everywhere

by Paul Moxness, Co-founder of The Always Care Consulting Company, Inc. and Coauthor of *Spin the Bottle Service: Hospitality in the Age of AI*

Paul Moxness had a 31-year career at Radisson Hotel Group as Global VP of Safety and Security and is a recipient of a Carlson Fellow, the company's highest individual honor. Paul is a Managing Partner at NorthPoint International, Director and Co-founder of Always Care Consulting, coauthor of the book *Spin the Bottle Service*, and professor at the Okanagan School of Business in Kelowna, Canada, where he lives with his wife, Kirsten.

In late January 2020, the first joint briefing about the novel coronavirus by British Columbia's Health Minister Adrian Dix and Provincial Health Officer Dr. Bonnie Henry was televised to the people of Canada's westernmost province. Two months later, the virus had taken hold, starting to spread from the densely populated areas of the lower mainland in and around the coastal city of Vancouver to many other parts of the province. Similar signs were being seen across the country, across the border in the United States, and across the world. The World Health Organization declared a global pandemic.

Be Kind, Be Calm, Be Safe

Dr. Henry and Minister Dix began giving daily briefings, and on March 17th a number of restrictions were introduced to try to control the virus' spread. After telling people to prepare for what could be a long and difficult journey ahead, Dr. Henry closed her update with what soon would become a catchphrase for people across the province: "Be kind, be calm, be safe."

As someone who has worked in security and crisis management for many years, it piqued my interest that she chose those words. I suggested to my wife that Dr. Henry might have had military training or, at least, a good background in dealing with long-term crises. As it turned out, she had both. She had been a military doctor, and she'd also dealt with pandemic outbreaks in Canada and abroad as part of her public health duties and via the World Health Organization. She knew that strict rules, regulations, and enforcement might not be enough to sustain the desired effects when a crisis dragged on. Motivating people to reflect on their behavior might.

Getting Pulled In

In the late summer of 2020, someone I didn't know and had never met tagged me in a post about The Kindness Games. The post was a brief video featuring the founders of TKG, Tim Wenzel and Lee Oughton. I watched it. It was basically bantering between two friends. They talked about how the world needed more kindness, and they gave shout-outs of gratitude to people they felt had shown them or others kindness.

The next day, they tagged me in another post. The day after that, they tagged me in yet another, and then another the following day. Although I didn't know them, it was clear they both worked in the security industry. I visited their profiles and discovered a number of common connections. The international security profession is a relatively small community, and the contacts we shared were people I knew and trusted. Although my security career was in a global hospitality company, my wife said she wasn't surprised it was security people behind The Kindness Games. She had always found our friends in the security profession to be inclusive, welcoming, and kind.

On September 14, 2020, having reviewed a number of The Kindness Games posts Lee and Tim had made, I really started to understand the value and potential for doing good that the burgeoning movement had. I wanted to join in, so I sent a brief note to Lee and Tim thanking them for starting the initiative and asking for tips on how to get started. Less than 15 minutes later, Lee answered. Within a couple hours, Tim chimed in, and within a couple days, I had posted my first video.

It lies in the nature of the term, but any movement — including one as good and compelling as The Kindness Games — is totally dependent on the contributions of its participants. Although I posted a few videos right off the bat, I let life distract me, and my contributions dried up. Tim, Lee, and others continued to tag me in their posts. Either they just didn't bother editing the list of hashtags and people that they pasted into each post, or they hadn't given up on me.

By November, I was getting frustrated with myself for not following up and completing the 30-post-challenge that would have made me an alum.

November is a month of remembrance, with Veterans Day in the United States and Remembrance Day in the United Kingdom and Canada. For me, that was the spur I needed to get my participation in The Kindness Games back on track.

Getting Back on Track

I like to say that I had a four-decade-long, post-high-school gap year in Europe that included a 31-year career at a company that didn't want to hire me. When I applied for my first job as a hotel security guard, the manager had said I was too old and too educated. When I'd tried to defend my position, he said I had too many opinions. As luck would have it, there was only one other applicant. That person withdrew, so despite my obvious shortcomings — old, educated, and with no military or law enforcement background — I was hired.

I was indeed unqualified for that first, line-level job. But from day one and throughout my career, people in professional networks and organizations have helped me plug gaps and fill shortcomings. One of those organizations was the Overseas Security Advisory Council (OSAC) at the US State Department.

November is also the month OSAC holds its annual briefing. Just as they had helped me throughout my career, they also helped me get my Kindness Games journey rolling again. I gave shout-outs to OSAC, to the OSAC Hotel Security Working Group, and then other public-private partnerships like those led by the UN, including the OSCE. Every video I posted triggered memories of other people who had shown me kindness and support along my path both in life and in my career. In December 2020, I was able to post video number 30. I completed The Kindness Games challenge!

In 1992, Joe Jacobi was one half of the C2 slalom team that won the first-ever Olympic Gold Medal for the United

States in whitewater kayaking. Joe knows all about finishing first. Yet, if you ask him, he believes starting lines are much more important than finish lines. Once you've crossed the starting line, you have opportunities to improve, to correct your course, and to make a difference. When you cross the finish line, it's over.

Joe likes to view finish lines as if they're starting lines. You can't change the outcome of the race, but you can start something new. With every starting line you cross, there lie endless opportunities to adjust your course and improve your journey.

Starting Now

When I uploaded post number 30 for The Kindness Games, I crossed a new starting line. The starting line to overtime, and the starting line that has provided the opportunity to take the games to new formats and new audiences.

To me, The Kindness Games is about much more than posting videos and shout-outs on social media. It has helped me become more aware of the value of kindness in my own behavior, and more importantly, it has also helped me become more conscious of the kindness of others.

It can be easy to feel overwhelmed by the seemingly insurmountable divisiveness that's visible in society. But dig a little deeper, and you'll find that beyond the noise, kindness is everywhere.

This quote is from a poem I wrote in my annual greeting to friends, family, colleagues, competitors, and counterparts a good number of years ago:

> *Problems aren't solved by heads stuck in sand.*
> *We need to engage and to reach out a hand!*
> *For we live in a world that we all have to share,*
> *And that, my dear friend, is why we must care.*

My hope is that what started as an online challenge between two people and morphed into a wider movement will help to amplify, promote, and continue to spread the message that kindness is contagious. It's contagious, it's inclusive, and it's free. There's no starting line. There's no finish line. There's always an opportunity to continue The Kindness Games through our daily behavior. All we have to do is care. Always Care.

Chapter 14: Agent of Change

by Wanda L. Townsend, Author, Coach, and Speaker

Wanda Townsend is an author, coach, and speaker. She's driven by her calling of "Teaching to Change Lives." For three decades she has been energized by helping former employers transform their cultures through emotional intelligence training, neuroscience research, and leader development. Wanda was a contributing author for *The Future Female Leader: Preparing Girls & Women to Lead the World* and *The New Next: International Leadership for Women*.

Created in September 2020 by Tim Wenzel and Lee Oughton, "The Kindness Games was started as a way to counter program the disruption, hate, and discontent that has engulfed our world during the COVID-19 Pandemic." If the global pandemic wasn't bad enough, shortly after its start we witnessed the unfolding of racial tension and civil unrest that spread like wildfire through the United States. To add to this already overwhelming situation, I found myself suddenly unemployed and confined to my home, obeying Washington state's stay-at-home order. Like many others,

I was gripped with anxiety, fear, and uncertainty. I spent countless hours watching the news and surfing the web to hear the latest updates on the pandemic, protests, and riots. Finally, I had to say, "Enough!"

All I longed for was a shimmer of positivity and healing — personal healing from the mental distress I felt and healing for the communities destroyed by conflict and injustice. In 2020, the whole country was bearing witness to a great deal of suffering with no end in sight.

Jumping In

My heart grieved for humanity. I knew I needed to take some type of action, but how could I in a world locked down? My search for positivity and kindness was found on LinkedIn of all places when I began following The Kindness Games. I watched curiously as various leaders recognized others with words of kindness and admiration. The impact of their posts was huge for my personal well-being. After roughly five months of sitting on the sidelines, I decided to raise my hand in spring 2021 and say, "Let's do this!" So, I contacted Tim Wenzel and told him I was ready to take on his challenge.

My Kindness Games journey launched when I met up with Tim over Skype. I thought we would have a casual conversation about the challenge, and he would go over expectations. But nope. Tim asked, "Are you ready?" I thought, duh, that's why we're having this meeting. But Tim continued, "Do you have someone in mind? Because I'm getting ready to hit record." You need to be careful around Tim Wenzel, he's a sly one and will push you off the cliff when you're least expecting it. I guess that's why I have so much respect for the man.

Anyway, after I jumped in (or rather, was pushed) with both feet, my next item of business was to sit quietly and deeply reflect on my personal life and professional career. I had five decades of memories to mull over. As I recalled previous life events, I found myself reimmersed in my experiences. Once forgotten images of old friends and coworkers rose to the forefront. My brain's hippocampus provided visions of leaders who "gave a damn" and who had a significant impact on my life and career. As individual faces appeared, I ferociously added their names to my list of people I wanted to make sure I recognized for their impact on my life.

Then came my reflection of emerging leaders. I asked myself, "Who are those individuals who could use a confidence boost or a boost in expanding their professional network? Who are the up-and-comers I know?" Surprisingly, many of them were family members: my three sons (ages 24, 19, and 18), a niece (a registered nurse), and a nephew (a police officer) working as first responders amidst the COVID-19 pandemic.

Old acquaintances whom I hadn't spoken to in years also flooded my memories. I spent a great deal of time sitting and reminiscing about how I first met these individuals. I could vividly see the places and rooms where we met and clearly recall the profound and meaningful conversations we had. It was such a gift to sit with the fond memories of our time together. I even went as far as to dig up old pictures I had that captured special moments we had shared together. Going down memory lane brought so much peace. It reminded me that kindness, love, compassion, and hope do exist.

How to Take Action

My Kindness Games journey provided me with several insights that I would like to share. I hope that one or two will resonate with you and nudge you into taking some type of action to spread love and kindness to those who need it most.

We Can't Go through Life Alone

I wish I had understood this in my 20s and 30s. If I had, perhaps my life would have been a more leisurely ride. We are not meant to go it alone. Humans are highly social beings, driven by a desire for community and belonging — hence my attraction to the TKG community. I now have a new pod of loving, caring, and supportive individuals to glide through life with. TKG offers a place where you never have to go it alone ever again.

We Have a Responsibility to Lift One Another

During 2020 and 2021, life was hard. Most people were obeying the stay-at-home, social distancing, and self-isolation policies put in place due to the global pandemic. The side effects of these policies on our physical and mental well-being have been significant. Businesses were forced to shut down, and unemployment skyrocketed. Schools closed, and parents and children alike found themselves navigating feelings of anxiety and uncertainty. Life as we knew it had instantly changed, almost overnight.

The Kindness Games provided a mental break from the chaos that had struck our individual and collective worlds. I found it extremely comforting to watch individuals lift one another up through kind words, inspiring videos, and beautiful imagery. It provided a break from the overwhelm that had taken over our world. It was incredibly fascinating to watch the response of those who had been lifted up with kindness and recognized in a shout-out. Many replied something to the effect of, "I really needed this today." "You don't know how much your post means to me." "I had no idea I made that much of an impact on you." The Kindness

Games was a reminder that humanity would prevail in the darkness.

Say Thank You to Those Who Made a Difference in Your Life

TKG pushed me to reflect on those who shared their time, energy, expertise, mentorship, and wisdom with me throughout my life. Thanking them was a small act of kindness that didn't cost anything. I was able to thank several family members, friends, former coworkers, former bosses, even people I only just met. One video I posted was about one of my lieutenants from nearly 30 years ago. This man has long retired from law enforcement, and we haven't seen each other in over 15 years. But the impact he had on me as a young trooper is forever in my heart and mind. TKG allowed me to recall the difference this individual made in my life and how his mentorship and friendship ultimately helped shape my professional leadership journey. But more importantly, it allowed me to thank him and share the impact he had on my life with the world.

Have Compassion for Others and Love Them Deeply

Kindness requires grace and compassion. Kindness does not judge. We have each lived stories that brought us to where we stand today. Some of those stories are about pain and suffering, but many are joyful blessings. During my Kindness Games journey, I found myself brimming with love and compassion for a group of individuals I have only met online. We continue to walk in community with one another long after our Kindness Games Challenge comes to a close.

Chapter 15: The Propagative Powers of Kindness

by Elisa Mula, MS

Elisa Mula formed the consulting business EM Designs, LLC in 2004 to challenge existing paradigms in business management. With a decade in physical security, Elisa has expanded her knowledge of video surveillance, access control, biometrics, and artificial intelligence, and how these technologies play a role in developing best practices within security programs. Elisa serves as the Executive Director for Moms in Security, a non-profit that supports those on the front lines fighting child trafficking and exploitation.

I was first introduced to The Kindness Games when I saw Mandy Myers and Bert Hart share a post about the initiative, but I had no clue how to "play." I assumed it was a milder version of the Ice Bucket Challenge, so I just started posting on Linkedin and giving people shout-outs.

This might be in part due to my Italian heritage, but in my very first post, I committed to donating 30 days' worth of food to our local homeless shelter. Italians love to feed people. It's how we show kindness.

Not realizing that 30 days of games really meant 30 days of kind social media posts, I nominated a few ladies to continue the game, made my food pantry donation, and went on my way. Once I realized I had not played the games correctly, I was on a mission to post an additional 30 videos to social media. The continuous process of cultivating kindness for 30 straight days shifted my perspective in so many ways. And the timing couldn't have been more perfect for that mindset shift.

Trying Again

Months after I had first responded to Mandy and Bert's post, I started making more video shout-outs and connected with the Kings of Kindness, Tim and Lee. These two were the catalyst. However, each and every individual who participated in The Kindness Games have just been amazing.

Looking back over the months of posts I made, there are some that meant more than others. My most popular post was probably a toss-up between the image of Maroon 5 laying on the floor with a child with special needs at a concert and Ashton Kutcher putting his career on hold to speak in front of Congress about the epidemic of human trafficking. Of course, these posts were not about people I knew personally, but they had inspired a level of kindness within me that I felt compelled to share with the world. And it was clearly well received by the larger community. People I never met began to comment and connect with me through these posts.

My most meaningful post was about my dad, the kindest man I've ever known. When my dad was dying, the hospital wouldn't allow me up to the room to see him. Hospitals wouldn't let anyone in during the pandemic, and we had no idea if he would make it out. I wasn't sure if I would ever get to tell him all the things a daughter needs to say to the man who has made her feel so loved and protected her whole life. So, I wrote it all down in a note, made sure the note got to him, and FaceTimed him from the hospital parking lot while he read it. That phone call is a memory I'll never forget. I still have the note.

My dad was a first responder and a certified first responder trainer. I still have his lesson plans and certificates in my office. He was generous and selfless. Even the word "kind" doesn't do him justice. When he died in August 2020, I knew how lucky I was to be his daughter and to have known him for 43 years. The Kindness Games gave me an opportunity to honor him in a cathartic way that I needed so badly during one of the bleakest years I can remember.

Kindness-Inspired Work

After many years of preparation, I launched my own security consulting business, EM Designs, in 2019. I'd formed the LLC in 2009 and received my first Woman Business Enterprise certification in 2012. It had taken me this long to feel ready and able to offer something of value to the community.

In early 2020, I won a project that would've put my business on the map in Manhattan. It was an opportunity to work with one of the major construction companies in New York City on a long-term project. And then the lockdowns started, effectively cutting off our momentum. That year forced me to take on work that felt incredibly inauthentic to who I was, making me devalue my efforts to a point where I considered closing our doors.

My story really wasn't that different from anyone else who was self-employed during COVID-19. And to be quite honest, my life really wasn't bad at all. I wasn't worried about losing my home, and my children were happy and healthy. So, at the end of the day, the only thing keeping me awake at night was thoughts about how to keep EMD going. I had to re-strategize and reinvent over and over just to stay afloat. But this was also the year I found The Kindness Games. Without taking a single day off, I networked virtually, researched, and cold-called so many people to try and find new, inventive ways of making business connections during the most uncertain time of my career. One of those connections was Lee Oughton.

Lee had shared a bit of his story with me, and while he is in a phenomenal place with his career and his business, something in his story really resonated with me: the idea of helping people in any way you possibly can, being passionate about kindness, and caring for others. That's what I was missing! Lee lives this every day. The man literally sends people messages on a daily basis just to check in and let them know that someone believes in them. This was how I was going to release the stress I was carrying about my business. Instead of trying to force things to change, instead of working hard at "fixing" anything, I was going to focus on people who really needed help. People who needed protecting. That's what my dad always did. And that's what I love about the security industry.

Lee inspired me to launch a nonprofit organization to go after the issue of human trafficking. I'd been following the issue for quite some time, learning from some of my contacts at Homeland Security and the FBI about the gap between what law enforcement can do jurisdictionally and what smaller organizations can do for children at risk. The idea that I could possibly be stressed out about business when my children are safe and happy at home was simply ridiculous. Then to think that there were children around the world in some of the worst conditions anyone could possibly imagine — well, this was the wake-up call I needed.

The very next day I started digging in and researching all the organizations that go out and rescue children around the world. Then I called on three superwomen for a little help. We're all moms with children that are safe, healthy, and happy, and we're all passionate about security. I asked them to join me in taking on the massive issue of human trafficking. How can we help end this? How can we protect them? And they jumped right in.

I started to ask this question over and over: "Who do you protect?" I launched Moms in Security with that question in my head. And it must be working, because some of the most incredible women in this industry decided to back me up in answering it. With the commitment of these amazing individuals, Moms in Security is an initiative inspired by The Kindness Games and fueled by a passion for protecting the most vulnerable.

When you use kindness, when you genuinely care for others, all the good things in life hunt you down. This is not to say that I don't still face challenges, but this shift in perspective has been life changing for me. The most important thing I've learned in my 43-year journey is that kindness starts from within but boomerangs back with intensity. Maybe you need to experience it to fully understand. But if my business never makes another dime, protecting others and protecting children will always be my mission, and The Kindness Games will forever be ingrained in my DNA.

Kind Moms around the World. . . Unite!

I'll close with my vision for the future. While I will of course continue to actively grow my own business, I'm also actively increasing my efforts with Moms in Security. I'm on a mission to find like-minded parents, non-parents, and security professionals who want to make children around the world feel loved, cared for, and protected. My hope is to find a cadre of moms and other kindhearted individuals to form an army of ambassadors that want nothing more than to heal the world with kindness. I'm clearly running with the right crew already!

I recognize how incredibly fortunate I was to have been loved and protected growing up. This world needs a lot of healing, but if we can grow, love, and protect kind little humans, we can speed up this healing process in a single generation.

Chapter 16: Refuse to Sink

by Kathleen Fariss, Business Strategist & Coach,
Champion of Others and Causes

Kathleen Fariss is the co-founder and CEO of Fariss Coaching & Consulting and a certified coach. As a change agent of more than 25 years, Kathleen loves to develop strategies for personal and professional transformation at the individual and organizational levels. Her coaching approach is rooted in the reality that even though change is inevitable, leaders who are empowered to find their unique voices, speak their truths, and have access to resources can flourish in uncertain times.

In my career and life, I've learned many valuable lessons, and one of the most important ones is this: Most of us want to avoid feeling vulnerable. We spend our days running away from it, but that shouldn't be surprising. Think about it. Does anyone really want to be vulnerable? Does anyone wake up in the morning and think, "I wonder what kinds of weaknesses I'll discover about myself today?"

For a long time, I avoided facing my vulnerabilities. I was taught, like most of us are, that vulnerability is a sign of weakness. People who embark on a journey of development and growth often think the purpose of the journey is to get rid of their weaknesses, not understand them. But I've learned that's not true. Teachers like the professor and author Brené Brown helped me see that understanding is the most important part. Brown tells us that it's vitally important to "embrace the suck" as a part of your growth. In fact, I was ready to face my weaknesses and embrace them when I first heard about The Kindness Games. I didn't have a clear idea what TKG was or what its goals were, but it didn't matter; the moment I heard about it, I knew I wanted to get involved. A voice in my head said, "This is it. It's time to get vulnerable."

I wish I could say my brave decision to jump in with both feet and get involved with TKG was just a sign of my incredible spiritual maturity, but it wasn't. The simple fact is that the months before I heard about TKG had primed me for this decision. The timing couldn't have been more perfect, and the result couldn't have been more welcome. Let me give some background.

Embrace the Shift

I learned a useful saying from my dear friend Jenny Darroch, who is Dean of the Farmer School of Business at Miami University in Oxford, Ohio. "I will go back to go forward," she says, and I'm going to do the same thing here.

I first encountered The Kindness Games in the fall of 2020, but it makes more sense to start on March 17, 2020, a day when life changed for me and millions of people around the world. The coronavirus pandemic was changing all our lives and filling our plans with uncertainty. The biggest shift for me came when my boss told us that we all had to pack up our desks and prepare to work from home. It wasn't that I hadn't been in a WFH situation before — not to be confused with WTF, which is something I'm sure I said that day, too

— but this time I knew it was going to be different. Not only was I going to work from home, but so was everyone in my personal and professional network. All my peers, family, friends, and the community that had rallied around me and the good work I was doing were heading home into a new routine of isolation and social distancing.

The same was true of my support system at work, which was changing due to budget cuts, leadership changes, and operational shifts. I knew technology would help me compensate and maintain these vital connections, but I couldn't deny that it was going to be a loss for me. I had to roll with the changes, and so I decided to shift my mindset. I asked myself a key question: Okay, things aren't going to be the same now. What's still possible?

I treated the challenge of quarantine as I did any other situation in my career: I developed a strategy to onboard myself at home, and I identified the necessary tools I'd need to continue advancing the good work we were doing based on the plans we had developed as a team. I packed up my files, pens, monitors, computer, printer, work-in-progress board, etc. And then it really hit me: I wasn't going to have my team with me. Every day I was going to be alone inside my house. How was this really going to work? How would I continue to move forward, serve others, lead my team, and feel good about myself and our work in this new situation created by the pandemic? These questions pointed to my own vulnerabilities, which the quarantine would soon force me to face.

Weather the Storm

At that point I did what anyone should do — I decided to ask for help. But it was clear the cavalry wouldn't be coming to my rescue anytime soon. Everyone else was struggling with similar challenges and trying to figure out how to move themselves and their work forward, too. You have no choice but to pivot — but how? What does that actually mean? I realized I was overthinking the situation. As I'd learned from reading Brené Brown's books, the stories we tell ourselves — especially the negative ones that come up when obstacles do — can become our reality if we give them life.

I was two months into working at home and wrestling with this situation when George Floyd was killed on May 25th, and civil unrest and protests against racial injustice boiled over across the nation. Change, first and foremost, is personal, and that tragic day (and the days that followed) made me want to speak out and stand up for others. But each time I took a step forward in this direction, I got in my own way again. I allowed myself (because I have since learned I have a choice) to be silenced, and that's when my anger, anxiety, and depression set in. What had happened to my community? What had happened to the world? What had happened to the families of everyone directly impacted by that day? What had happened to me?

Feeling so powerless shone a spotlight on my own vulnerabilities again. I couldn't avoid them, but I realized that I could choose to focus on what I could control: my self-talk, my energy, my self-care, my focus, my movements — in other words, my life. I realized I had a responsibility to hold myself accountable and take care of myself; if I did that, then I'd be able to care for and support others. If I didn't — if I gave in to feelings of helplessness — I wouldn't be able to be of service to anyone at all. I have always thrived in supporting others and championing causes, and I realized how much I wanted to continue being a part of something bigger than myself. I didn't know what that "something" even was, though. But as it turned out, it was right around the corner.

Put on the Life Vest

There's no way to stop change; it's inevitable. Shift happens. Flash forward months later, and I was participating in a Whole and Intentional Leadership Development (WiLD) call led by Dr. Rob McKenna and Dr. Daniel Hallak. WiLD's mission is to invest in leaders like me to support our personal and professional growth, so we can own our leadership roles and lead from a space of wholeness. Not long after that call, Daniel posted a video on LinkedIn about something called The Kindness Games. I respect Daniel and Rob so much, and I deeply value their work, so I was intrigued. I had no idea what the rules or goals of The Kindness Games were, but I decided to jump in and start posting in September 2020 anyway. I didn't think it mattered; I had found a space where I could learn to be vulnerable, "embrace the suck," and post videos recognizing people who'd had an impact on me. I was ready to join a community and become part of something I felt was bigger than me and would introduce me to a larger world and new opportunities for growth. (Notice I said "felt" and not "thought," because I was tapping into something besides reason and logic here.)

That decision was a powerful one. It forced me to look around and try to identify the people — the role models — whose good work and social impact had inspired me, many of whom had demonstrated another important lesson: Learning while doing is often what the best leaders do. I turned to LinkedIn and started reading all about TKG's founders, Tim Wenzel and Lee Oughton; I wanted to know more about the story behind why they had started The Kindness Games. It was an incredible effort that had started out between two individuals who had never met in person, who gave shout-outs to leaders they admired and respected. It seemed so simple and clear. What did they hope to achieve? The by-product of their efforts was something wonderful: Leaders who were recognized would experience the kinds of affirmations and organic healing that would make them better able to go out into their communities and support healing there.

Learn to Swim

Cell phone cameras have been around for more than 20 years, and the technology is easy enough for anyone to use. But that didn't matter — I still experienced plenty of trouble when I started making my videos. It had nothing to do with the technology, though; I was super uncomfortable with sharing my voice at all, especially when the camera started. When I first started recording videos for The Kindness Games, it took me somewhere between 10 to 15 takes because I didn't know what to say or how to say it. And then, of course, I wondered if anyone would even watch the video. (In personal coaching, such discomfort and hesitation always presents you with a chance to ask your client something like, "Would you like to unpack that?" or, "What do you think is behind that?")

After I'd posted a few times, Tim Wenzel reached out and invited me to a "Get to Know You" Zoom call, and I was so excited. I thought, "Wow, he reached out to me. Little old me?!"

We jumped on a call, and near the end he said, "Are you ready?"

"For what?" I asked. The red recording button suddenly went on, and off we went.

That first Zoom recording with Tim went off without a hitch. It was magical and healing for me. Yes, I did feel at moments like I was going to throw up, but I kept taking deep breaths and giving myself permission to share my voice as it was. On that video I recognized a leader who had impacted me and the lives of others. As I look back on that moment now, I am forever grateful to Tim, even if I had been in-TIM-idated (as one of my peers joked) at the time. He encouraged me, provided a space for me to have a voice, and welcomed me into the The Kindness Games family.

Swim on Your Own

The new path I was on when I became involved with The Kindness Games felt right — like it was exactly where I was supposed to be — and odd at the same time. I started connecting with other participants and then jumped on a Zoom call with Lee Oughton. After hearing his life-changing story, I felt like The Kindness Games community truly were my people, my tribe, my family, and a group I could lean into and support as I continued to learn and grow along the way.

I was in this happy state when another wave, another major change took place in my life — one that was just as impactful as quarantine or the social protests. This time, though, the change didn't come from an external source; it came directly from me. I decided to leave my nine to five job and put all of my energy into my coaching and consulting work. This meant I was leaving another community — one I had known for over 10 years. Here was another shift in my life, another loss to grieve.

I felt a great deal of support and love when I made this momentous decision. Some of the best advice and feedback I received at this point came from a leader I respected a great deal, Kristen Andersen Daley. Kristen has been a steadying presence in my professional life — always calm, balanced, and understanding in every situation. I asked her how she managed to maintain this balance, how she kept her compassionate poker face in every meeting, all the time. Her response provided me with another step in my own journey. She said she worked hard to remain constant (not too high and not too low) so that she could provide the best support possible to her team. What an epiphany!

Remain Constant through the Shifts

It was a struggle to reach my early TKG goal of 30 posts in 30 days, and I gave myself permission to take extra time to complete them. Tim was thoughtful and supportive as he watched me work on this; he suggested I complete the posts by Thanksgiving and then take a few weeks off. In hindsight, I can see what he was doing. This was his kind way of encouraging me to pause, allow myself time to heal through the change and loss I was experiencing, and then pivot back in December for overtime postings. I thought that was a brilliant idea, and I spent that time healing and finding a way to remain constant at the same time.

I love networking and, as anyone who knows me can surely attest, I love humans. I love just being around them. As I rested and recharged after Thanksgiving, I thought about serving the world, TKG, my community, my family, and myself. What was next? What should I do? The answer seemed obvious: I could continue posting, continue reaching out and inviting others to participate, and do my part in moving TKG forward. Why was this so important to me? Because being kind matters. Kindness heals others and it heals ourselves. When we are given access to the resources needed to heal us and help us lead, it makes us open and willing to do the tough inside work that's necessary to grow. When that happens, anything is possible.

So on I went: reaching out to others, meeting new friends, and holding space for those who needed support. Out of this intentional effort blossomed several deep relationships, including with Janina Lincke, Kehkashan Dadwani, Kelsey Carnell, Kunle Pelemo, Tim, Lee, and many others. My Kindness Family. I would never have had the opportunity to welcome these individuals into my life if it weren't for TKG.

Making an effort to be a part of the TKG community allowed us to rally around something much bigger than ourselves. The benefits of being on Zoom — and so in other people's homes and offices — enabled us to become more vulnerable, learn, and grow. It helped us build momentum behind TKG, so it evolved from what I like to think of as a "bro challenge" into a global healing effort that moves mountains, helps leaders break generational cycles, and finds something new.

Insights from the Journey

I feel so blessed to have my Kindness Games family of leaders, who come from all over the globe and have joined together to learn and grow and be of service to others. Collectively our journey has been one of self-discovery, growth, inside-out work, and going first. Leading is hard work, and at times it can be lonely, too. But what other choice do we have? We just have to give a damn, lean in, and keep our eyes on the goal of leaving the people we meet and support in a better place than when we first met them. That's our duty.

I want to close with some things I learned during this season of growth thanks to TKG and all the lovely and kind humans involved with this global effort. I hope other people will be helped by these insights just as so many people have helped me with theirs on my own journey.

You're Not Alone

In difficult or chaotic times, it's easy to withdraw because we feel like life is happening to us, rather than that we are making life happen. Remember that you're not alone in feeling this way. You are not alone in this journey. Be brave and take one step forward, regardless of what it is, and lean in. You'll be surprised by the outpouring of support you'll receive, and, in the process, you'll be helping others, too. We never know what others are going through when we take action. The most important thing is just to do something.

Asking for Help Is Courageous

Regardless of how you were raised or the leaders you followed in the past (and who maybe didn't model the best, healthy behavior) it's important to reach out and ask for help. Asking is not a sign of weakness. In fact, it takes great courage, strength, and a willingness to face your vulnerability to seek support.

Shift Happens

When you feel stuck in a situation, get moving — that includes moving your body. You have much more control over your destiny and the path forward than you probably think. Movement creates energy, and energy is vital to making changes. That includes your emotions. The emotions you activate when you start shifting yourself and moving can also shift the next step you'll take.

And remember: inaction is also a choice. That's why in every situation, holding ourselves accountable to ourselves, our family, and our community is not only important, but also our responsibility.

Stay in Community

When you decide to go into hiding or dig a hole in the sand, you really aren't invisible to other people. As a coach of mine once pointed out, "If you're acting like an ostrich and hiding your head in the sand, we can still see your rear end." Your community is there for you, and you can access it at any time. Pick up the phone, send an email, schedule a Zoom call, meet for coffee, and stay connected. Your community needs you to share your love and light as much as you need that from your community.

Have Faith

Believing in a cause much bigger than you requires first believing in yourself. You have to remind yourself that you are valued, you are enough, and you are worthy. You matter. Later, when you become involved in that bigger cause and have the necessary support, you can help others around you become involved, too.

Your Voice Matters: Share It!

When we choose to share our voices, we can be seen and heard. When we are seen and heard, we break restricting cycles and generational norms. We can heal through the language that we've shared. How do you do this? Start with small steps: practice using your voice in smaller ways and in safe spaces first. It's like exercise or building a new muscle. It's better to build up gradually. Identify the tools, safe spaces, and practices you need to find your true voice.

Get Out of Your Own Way

We can shift and grow once we become more aware of the self-defeating behaviors we continue to display. That includes the triggers under the surface that cause us to spend our days on autopilot and the damaging shadow sides of our personality that threaten to sabotage our best-intended efforts. It's important to identify those harmful elements in our lives and address them, saying, "I see you, and you are not going to control me and keep me chained in the past for the rest of my life." We must choose not to give them any more energy or power. This is a learned behavior that requires much practice and patience.

Be Curious

Curiosity and listening to yourself go hand in hand. Ask yourself what to do each time your intuition is telling you something. Keep asking yourself questions about why this is happening. Stay curious, and never doubt what your intuition wants you to see. There is learning that can take place in that moment, and it's our job to figure out what the lesson is. Don't hesitate to ask others about what you are feeling, either. When you have more information, you can make better decisions about the path ahead of you.

Get a Coach or Mentor

We're all leaders, and as we move into different chapters of our lives, we not only need family and friends to show up for us differently, but we also need to show up differently for ourselves. It's important to ask yourself what support you need that you maybe didn't need before, and it's okay to not know the answer. An important part of the journey is sometimes being comfortable with not knowing what you don't know.

This goes back to my earlier comments about the importance of vulnerability and recognizing that sometimes you're the one with the least amount of information in the room. That's why leaders must invest in their leadership. Hire a coach or get a mentor to help with your development both professionally and personally. It's not a sign of weakness. The reality is we all need support to continue leading our own lives, as well as leading through others, to move the good work forward.

Celebrate All That's Special and Unique about You

When we reflect on ourselves and write out all that's unique and special about us, we start to find patterns. When that happens, we're able to make important changes. We can shift to kindness or gratitude or being focused on others. This exciting transformation takes place when we begin owning our stories and honoring all that is unique about us.

KEY TAKEAWAYS

Change Your Mindset, Change Your World

1   Create your community.
Look for those who want to express themselves positively, while at the same time are willing to engage in bold, honest, and judgement-free conversations.

2   Help others feel a sense of belonging.
There's enough food for us all to eat, and there are plentiful seats at the table for us to sit together. We can't allow discrimination or polarization to creep into our lives.

3   We heal through our communities.
Lean on your connections with others during difficult times. The only way through is together.

4   Inspire and uplift.
You don't have to think too hard or overdo it. Keep it short, simple, from the heart, and always authentic.

Wrap Up & Resources

Conclusion

Someone once asked me, "Are leaders responsible for how people perceive and experience them?"

The conversation was about people who didn't want to get along with the team. People who seemed to want to be unhappy. You know people like this. This question was meant to point out the fact that no matter our intentions, no matter how amazing we are, we can't always get everyone aligned. Some people don't want to join the culture we're building or follow the vision we're casting. There are people who will always choose not to understand. Some will always mock, always pointing to our faults or the exceptions, which somehow invalidates the rest of the evidence we're building our project upon.

Some people will never have a day of fun in their entire life, because they choose it and wish it upon those around them as well.

I answer, "Yes. We're responsible for how people perceive and experience us as leaders. This journey, for me, is worth the struggle."

Everyone leads in some way. We all have people who watch us. All of us have people who look to us for guidance and strength. What would change if you aspired to lead with kindness?

Beyond The Kindness Games

September 2021 marked the one-year anniversary of The Kindness Games. Mike Gips unknowingly became the 30th TKG Alumni on the day of our first anniversary. Over 200 people were participating and the security industry had fully taken notice. The leadership and coaching industry was quickly becoming the second largest demographic within our community and is now rivaling the security industry as the prime audience and participant base.

Soon companies asked if we put on programs. Wellness, employee engagement, leadership, and culture initiatives became a part of what we do. We host online workshops so individuals could learn business skills that help them lead with kindness more effectively in this crucial environment. The Kindness Games went from a game played on LinkedIn to a leadership and wellness company, helping others empower and uplift their sphere of influence.

The stories you've read here are but a sample of the stories that came out of our first year. As *The Kindness Games: How a Single Post Changed Our Mindset About Community* is released, we're embarking on our third year of healing communities and changing the world by leading with kindness.

I would love to tell you that the X is confined to the war zones and executive protection assignments Lee and I have lived, but it's not true. TKG Alumni and participants have endured backlash for their choice to infuse their communities with kindness. The simple act of uplifting another has drawn scorn. For uplifting someone who may be hurting for their world to admire, we have been called hypocrites, do-gooders, and out of touch.

TKG participants have been told by their managers to "stop posting and contributing to The Kindness Games if you want to work here." They have been questioned by colleagues and mentors, "Do you really want to be known as a The Kind Professional?" They've been admonished to "think about what future employers will think about these childish, idyllic posts in a few years."

Rob McKenna had a conversation with me shortly after TKG started to catch on. He warned that this was quite countercultural. It threatened establishments and people of influence. It threatened to unseat a source of intimidation-based power. But Rob wasn't warning me off. He was smiling. He was making sure that I was intentionally choosing this struggle. He was welcoming a brother to the fight. This journey for us is worth the struggle.

Many TKG-ers have come to Lee and me with their dilemmas. We tell them all the same thing. "This is your choice and your life. We would never tell you what to do, and we will never look down on you for the path you choose. Choices have consequences. But consider this, do you want to work, lead, and live in this environment?"

It's a sad testament to the state of the world we live in. Helping and uplifting others creates discontent. It's the dangerous societal shift to a faceless, human-less society where we all should find a box that makes us happy and stay in it. It's clear that we should not be influencing across communities, because it's a disruption to the power dynamics which began in earnest with the COVID-19 pandemic. Stay in your box, with your people, and your ideas and be happy. This is what we're being told in a threatening manner.

In what world would you like to work, lead, and live? In what world will you raise the next generation? What world will you leave behind?

It's your choice and ultimately your struggle.

Some have chosen to stop contributing to The Kindness Games. That's fine. They're still friends. We love them. But as we continue to see them, the dissatisfaction hasn't faded. Their struggle hasn't ceased. Some have come to realize they've chosen an "easier" struggle, which is unfulfilling.

Some TKG-ers have chosen to begin looking for new opportunities, new environments to work in, or new communities to take part in, to find or build a place they want to live life in. Good for them. You shouldn't have to remain in a toxic environment. You should be free to be curious, to learn and to grow.

Then there are those who have chosen to smile and remain in troubled waters. To continue to do great work, to lead with kindness, to aspire to be a force of change within an organization or a community that's less than appreciative. They have chosen to endure the temporary hardship on behalf of the watchers. To show those on the sidelines that you can live your values, values which uplift everyone around you. You can upset the status quo in a way which inspires instead of destroys. While some may succeed in changing these environments, all of them will forever change the people within them. Because once you've seen altruistic courage, once you've seen the conviction to make the world a measurably better place despite the backlash, you can't forget it. You may ignore it for a while, but the truth will not let you go. The happy sacrifice made by someone who desires to serve a purpose greater than themself is an eternal testament which will not walk quietly into the night.

Lee and I have had numerous personal conversations with TKG participants who endured, who stayed the course in the face of backlash. All of them became an inspiration to some of the watchers in these environments. Some of them were able to rise above the haters and continue onward to better things. Yet a few actually melted the hearts of their critics. They endured through the accusation of hypocrisy and created believers.

So, they won?!
No, they healed.

They healed broken hearts and scarred minds. They showed people who were in pain, who had been traumatized by life, who had allowed emotional calluses to form as a defense, that it's okay to open up again. There's a way to lead which uplifts those around you. It's not safe. It involves vulnerability. But it is far from weakness. It has the power to transform lives, to illuminate ill intent, and to model an alternative, innocuous demonstration of strength.

We are absolutely responsible for how people perceive and experience us. We are not, however, responsible for how they respond to or talk about us. But we are responsible for how we engage with and influence others. We need to lead a life with clarity of purpose: to lead a life which empowers and uplifts those around us in an effort to heal our communities and change the world by leading with kindness. The endeavor of leading a life of holistic kindness can heal you as well. It can make you feel again. It can cause you to embrace the beauty and brokenness of humanity again.

The leading with kindness philosophy creates a roadmap we all can follow. We believe that leading with kindness is the strongest, most engaging and sustainable form of leadership available.

The story of the first year of The Kindness Games ends here. The next chapter is yours to write. Lee and I are looking forward to learning about your journey and how you've impacted your world.

Will you invite us to share your TKG journey?

List of Contributors

Kunle Pelemo

"Chapter 12: Kindness Is Contagious" on page 120

Angela Scalpello

"Chapter 4: The Power of Transformative Questions" on page 52

Christopher Stitt

"Chapter 7: Be the Light" on page 83

Brandon Tan

"Chapter 11: Recognize Your Impact" on page 115

Wanda L. Townsend

"Chapter 14: Agent of Change" on page 140

Heidi Tripp

"Chapter 2: Rediscovering Myself" on page 25

Glossary

Alumni — members of the TKG community that have completed their TKG Journey

Kindversaries — anniversaries of completed TKG Journeys for TKG Alumni

Overtime — additional 30-day journeys after the initial TKG Journey has been completed; first overtime "OT," second "2OT," third "3OT," and so on

TKG (The Kindness Games) — a social media challenge to post once a day for 30 days, each day recognizing someone who has impacted one's life postively

TKG Journey — the complete challenge of 30 posts in 30 days

Acknowledgements

Sarah-Marie Baumgartner

I'm grateful to all those who participate in The Kindness Games. It has been a bright spot in my life to know so many amazing people who truly care about humanity and how we all need each other to truly live a full life. I can't wait to see how this grows and the impact it has on the world. Thank you to Lee, Tim, Kathleen, Kelsey and Kehkashan for their leadership, encouragement and the time they pour into The Kindness Games and those that participate.

Kelsey Carnell

The Kindness Games was the epitome of a challenge that became a lifestyle and a movement. We have such an amazing community of alumni, and I have grown so much closer to the global team that we have. I'm empowered and motivated by each of them. I love that everyone has brought their own creativity to their 30 days and we have built such an amazing group of force multipliers that just "click." Anyone you meet — even for the first time — feels like a forever friend. I truly believe that I wouldn't have met this amazing group if it wasn't for TKG. We have a diverse group that comes from all over the globe, in all industries. Talk about the power of passion and networking.

Margo Cash

The Kindness Games turned out to be a major gift for myself as I gave kindness to others. I'm now on a personal journey of healing and growth and realization that I'm in control of my own happiness, destiny, and the energy in which I put out into the world. I'm so thankful and can't wait to continue my journey spreading kindness as I know this is only the beginning.

Kehkashan Dadwani

I have done many things in life, and I'm proud of my accomplishments. I can break my life into chapters and identify the moment when one chapter closed, and another began. The most recent chapter begins in October 2020. I got on a call with Tim Wenzel, joined The Kindness Games movement, and was invited to join the GSD Crew. A single moment in time shifted my trajectory and changed my life. I committed to always questioning the status quo, and taking charge of my destiny by joining a group of fierce professionals who are dedicated to evolving not only the Security industry, but the world.

Kathleen Fariss

I have undergone multiple industry and role transitions throughout my career, each presenting challenging and rewarding onboarding experiences. Yet, stepping into The Kindness Games and the security industry has been truly transformative. I owe this incredible journey to the visionary founders, Tim Wenzel, Lee Oughton, Kelsey Carnell, and Kehkashan Dadwani, whose leadership, courage, and commitment to investing in others have had a profound impact on me. Their recognition of my potential has made me feel seen and valued. The moment Tim invited me to join them in launching the LLC will forever hold a special place in my heart. Together, we have initiated a movement that encourages personal development and kindness in others, and I take great pride in being part of the TKG Community. I'm immensely grateful to Lee and Tim for their life-changing presence in my life. They have taught me the importance of embracing my authentic self, and I'm honored to be among the sacrificial leaders in the TKG community who are dedicated to making a positive difference in the world.

Sue Ginsburg

While I now pop in and out of TKG conversations, I'm always greeted with a warm welcome, and I always leave the conversation feeling lighter. TKG has absolutely been a silver lining of this pandemic for me! To Tim and Lee, a special shout-out for starting this movement and showing the world the domino effect kindness can have. To all my fellow Kindness Gamers, I'm proud to be your teammate.

Michael Gips

It would be unconscionable for me not to thank Lee Oughton, Tim Wenzel, and especially Lisa Oliveri for bringing me into the TKG family. Lee and Tim piqued my interest, and Lisa's participation drew me in for good. Thanks to the three of you and the entire TKG family!

Bill Massey

Thank you, Tim Wenzel and Lee Oughton for creating The Kindness Games and Tim, for that initial shout-out back in October 2020.

Paul Moxness

I'll likely never know why Lee and Tim tagged me in their posts during the early days of The Kindness Games. If they hadn't, in the endless stream of social media, I might have missed the opportunity to join the journey that introduced me to so many wonderful people and the value kindness contributes to the lives we live. I'll be forever grateful to Lee and Tim for the tags that touched me with their kindness.

Elisa Mula

These gamers and kindness alumni are some of the most important supportive and inspiring people I've ever met. I'm going to continue to lean on this community for advice, guidance, and support, but most of all inspiration and collaboration on how I can spread kindness to the world. I jumped into The Kindness Games at a point when I didn't realize just how much kindness I needed in my life. But the universe — and Tim and Lee — provided!

Kunle Pelemo

Special thanks to the amazing Tim Wenzel and Lee Oughton for creating TKG. At that point in time, the world needed to show and receive kindness more than ever before. The spark TKG created has become an explosion of kindness that has spread through many communities.

Angela Scalpello

I'm grateful to Tim and Lee who started The Kindness Games. I'm also grateful to everyone else who has joined in and continued the movement.

Christopher Stitt

Thanks to those that have helped me along my path and the chain that linked me to The Kindness Games community.

Brandon Tan

I would like to thank those who put this all together. Tim Wenzel, Lee Oughton, and Kathleen Fariss. The impact you all have made with The Kindness Games have been immeasurable. Because of this challenge, I have grown to be more confident and prepared to take on public speaking and spreading positivity virtually and in-person. Cheers!

Wanda L. Townsend

I am forever grateful to Tim Wenzel and Lee Oughton for creating TKG. My journey introduced me to extraordinary leaders who helped get me through one of the most challenging years in my lifetime. I have developed lasting friendships with people I probably wouldn't have ever met if it weren't for TKG. I had the privilege of sharing my voice, telling my story and introducing the world to other kind, thoughtful, and loving human beings. My hope in contributing to this book is for you to see that kindness exists and regain faith in our humanity.

Heidi Tripp

I wanted to do this because it was a little outside of my comfort zone and would force me to grow, because it aligned with my values and would hopefully help me build a skill I needed to continue to be successful at work. Plus, I thought it would be fun. I had no idea the community that existed around The Kindness Games or that I would feel so welcomed and supported. I am completely honored and humbled to be a part of this group of incredible people.

About the Authors

Lee Oughton

Lee Oughton is a Security, Risk, and Crisis Management Leader and co-founder of The Kindness Games. With experience in corporate and high-risk environments, Lee specializes in building programs and formulating policies and procedures designed to minimize exposure to risks, vulnerabilities, and associated consequences to enterprises. Lee influences high level decisions and builds relationships with executives, key decision makers, customers, and law enforcement agencies.

Dedicating his life to giving back to others and creating opportunities, Lee's a dedicated volunteer through many humanitarian organizations, including The Relentless Revival Safe Haven, a project to help victims of human trafficking. Lee dedicates his kind soul to his wife, parents, children, family, and other Kindness Crusaders. Originally from the UK, Lee now resides in Mexico with his amazing wife Ery.

Connect with Lee on LinkedIn: **h2c.ai/Lee**

Tim Wenzel

Tim Wenzel is a thought leader, sought after speaker in the Security, Leadership, and Wellness industries, and co-founder of The Kindness Games. With a passion to transform the existing paradigms of leadership and risk management while creating well designed programs, he's widely recognized as a SME in Enterprise Security Risk Management (ESRM). In 2022, Tim was named a Global Influencer and Thought Leader in the Security Industry by IFSEC International.

Tim is known for building high performing, autonomous teams and Leading with Kindness. As a highly regarded coach and mentor, Tim works with people of all ages, backgrounds, and industries to find their voice, cultivate their confidence, identify and overcome imposter syndrome, and to thrive within the organizations and cultures they find themselves.

Connect with Tim on LinkedIn: h2c.ai/Tim

Remember to add #TheKindnessGames
to your own TKG journey posts!

Printed in the USA
CPSIA information can be obtained
at www.ICGtesting.com
JSHW061426120124
55186JS00005B/56